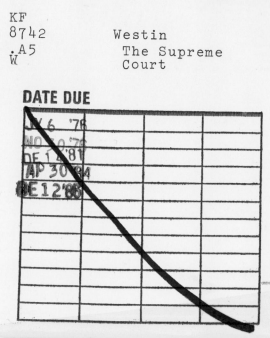

Edited by ALAN F. WESTIN

ASSOCIATE PROFESSOR OF PUBLIC LAW AND
GOVERNMENT, COLUMBIA UNIVERSITY
MEMBER OF THE DISTRICT OF COLUMBIA BAR

THE

SUPREME

COURT:

VIEWS FROM INSIDE

W. W. NORTON & COMPANY, INC. · *New York*

Contents

Preface

My greatest debt in assembling this collection is to the Justices of the Supreme Court who made copies of their printed or typescript addresses available to me: Chief Justice Earl Warren and Associate Justices Hugo Black, William O. Douglas, Felix Frankfurter, Tom C. Clark, John M. Harlan, William J. Brennan Jr., Charles E. Whittaker and Potter Stewart. While limitations of space made it impossible to include a speech by each of the present Justices and topical coverage sometimes required the choice of one speech and relegation of parallel speeches to the Bibliography, my understanding of the scope and tenor of judicial commentary was widened considerably by having read all of the speeches.

For assistance in collecting speeches of previous members of the Court, I am especially indebted to Mr. Justice Frankfurter and Mr. Justice Harlan, and to their respective secretaries, Elsie Douglas and Ethel McCall. Helen Lally of the Library of the Supreme Court and Morris Cohen, Associate Librarian of Columbia University Law School were most cooperative in the face of trying call-slips and queries. My wife, Bea, and Eleanor and Robert Miller aided me, to the straining of vocal chords, in the reading of manuscript and proofs.

Introduction:
On the View from Inside

John W. Davis, one of the masters of courtroom argument, once suggested in a lecture on the art of oral advocacy that this was a subject to be presented by judges, not by practicing lawyers. "Who would listen to a fisherman's weary discourse on fly casting," he asked rhetorically, "if the fish himself could be induced to give his views on the most effective method of approach?" A few years later, quoting Mr. Davis' remark, Justice Robert H. Jackson delivered a delightful and revealing lecture on "Advocacy Before the United States Supreme Court," billing the speech as "some meditations by one of the fish." Mr. Davis' quest for the inner perspective parallels the purpose of this short volume on the Supreme Court; Justice Jackson's willingness to speak about things other than lower-court reform and legal ethics signifies the tradition among Supreme Court members which makes this collection possible.

Our normal panorama of the Supreme Court comes from the formal opinions written by the Justices. A majestic "Affirmed" or "Reversed"—without further explanation—has never been the mode of judicial communiqué in this country. Since the Court's first decision in 1791, over 280,000 pages of majority, concurring, and dissenting opinions have undertaken to communicate what the Court did in the cases it decided, what it would not do, and why. Today, three bulky official volumes are required to print the opinions for a single year.

The general observer who reads these opinions carefully finds in them a wealth of data about judicial review in the American political system. He finds the lines of agreement and division

within the Court; the great debates of constitutional theory rever-
berating in the nation at large; the degree of rapport or tension between the Court and its governmental fellows—Congress, the
President, and the States; the tenderness or hostility of the federal
judiciary at a given moment toward the claims of groups such as
organized labor, business, Negroes, or Catholics; and the particular
economic, sectional, and social issues of each decade, from National
Banks and Fugitive Slaves to Taft-Hartley injunctions, Passport
Procedures, and School Segregation.

Even though the opinions open important vistas to us, they are
not exactly picture-windows opening onto the Supreme Court-
yard. The opinions present only a result, and because the Supreme Court does not deliberate in public, how that result was
reached remains cloudy. For many rational and irrational reasons,
American practice has determined that the bones of Justice—
even Constitutional Justice—are best shaken and thrown in a
darkened temple. Thus we see "before" and "after" at the Supreme Court but not "during." We can scrutinize what goes
before the Court—the trial record, with its documentary etching
of an unfolding dispute brought to law; the opinions of lower
courts; the briefs and oral arguments of the parties and their
friends; and the leading questions of the Justices while the case
is being argued. When the Justices rise and file out through the red
velour drapes behind the Bench, however, the curtain literally
falls across the Court's proceedings.

No outsider knows whether or what the Justices read in making
up their minds. The intra-Court debates are held behind the
locked doors of the Conference Room and no transcript is made.
The successive votes of each Justice on the cases which swing
back and forth within the Court are not revealed, so changes of
position can not be noted and analyzed as we are able to analyze
those of Congressmen. Only years later, when biographies of deceased Justices may be written, do we learn the significant changes
in wording and concept within the majority and dissenting opinions
as they progressed through various drafts and were circulated among
the "brethren." No systematic briefings or helpful leaks to the
press issue from the law clerks, as they do from executive or
legislative aides, and memoranda from the clerk to his Justice
remain confidential. Finally, the Justices do not submit to press

conferences, either to explain their opinions under questioning or to respond to the general queries of a press corps.

All of these key elements in the judicial process take place in private. Only when they have been completed do the curtains part again and the Justices come back to view. When the result in each case is announced by a spokesman for the majority, he lets slip what he chooses about the internal feuds or passions stirred by "No. 521" or "No. 16," to be matched, perhaps, by a statement in reply from one of the dissenters.

Following the Supreme Court, then, is like trying to assemble a picture puzzle for which several important pieces have been playfully withheld by the manufacturer. As a result, students of judicial review subject the formal opinions to a textual examination comparable to the dissection of Biblical passages, Platonic dialogues, and Marxist treatises. When the opinions have been milked dry, the searchers move on to expert commentary, judicial biographies, political histories, the tidbits of Washington columnists (almost invariably wrong or warped), the expansive recollections of former law clerks, or observations by law professors fresh from a convivial hour with Mr. Justice X. Some political scientists, frustrated at the secrecy of the Conference, turn to a kind of scholarly astrology to pierce the curtain: game theory—"assuming each Justice decides cases so as to win the deciding vote position for himself . . ."; or scalagram analysis—"isolating the factors which decide the case in a given area, translating these into mathematical terms, we can predict that if a case exactly like this ever comes up again . . ." and a host of other alchemist's techniques.

The surprising thing is that, apart from the quotation of passages from a few of the better-known addresses of the Justices, there has never been a systematic examination of what the Justices say in public about themselves and their agency of government. Especially surprising is the fact that a collection of contemporary commentary has never been assembled as a teaching guide about judicial review. It is the thesis of this volume that the self-image of the Justices and their comments about the work of the Court provide a useful supplementary tool for students. Like any tool, its proper use depends upon a correct understanding of its purposes, special qualities, and limitations.

First, it should be appreciated at once that the Justices speak

out *primarily* to advance the prestige of the Supreme Court and
defend it against critics. No Justice has taken the rostrum to urge
elimination of judicial review of legislation. No Justice has supported popular election for members of the Court, or periods
of limited rather than life tenure. No Justice has urged the institution of devices short of constitutional amendment to override
judicial rulings holding legislative acts unconstitutional, such as
national referenda or a two-thirds re-passage of an act by Congress. No Justice in recent decades has called for an increase
in the Court's number of members, or for a compulsory re-
tirement age to prevent the creep of senility on the bench. No
Justice has supported Congressional limitations on the Court's
appellate jurisdiction—not in the 1820's as to review of state
court decisions or public land cases, nor in the 1890's as to
municipal bond or railroad cases, nor in the 1950's as to segregation, loyalty-security, or passport matters.

Each of these positions which none of the Justices has endorsed
has had eloquent champions among our leading political figures,
from Thomas Jefferson and Theodore Roosevelt to Senator Robert
LaFollette, Franklin Roosevelt, and the platoon of influential
Senators and Congressmen pressing for "court-curbs" in 1958.
Had the men who served as Justices since 1790 not gone on the
Court, but performed as Senators, Governors, Attorneys-General,
Professors or Presidents, it is possible that quite a few of them
would have associated themselves publicly with one or another of
the reform proposals. And, Justices who have retired from the
Court *have* advocated changes in the Court's numbers or jurisdiction. But, as members of the Court, the Justices speak
entirely on the defensive on what might be called "institutional
questions"—those touching the nature of the judicial Establishment. This could be predicted, of course. Men elevated to the
post of Master Architects of a society should not be expected to
endorse the idea of "do-it-yourself" blueprints.

Thus one major purpose and function of speeches by the Justices has been to defend the Court from serious onslaughts, as
openly as the canons of propriety in each era would permit.
Minor defenses are also part of the pattern. The first Justice
John Marshall Harlan went to great pains in an 1896 address[1] to
advise the Bar and the public that there were no such things as

[1] "The Supreme Court and Its Work," 30 *American Law Review* 900 (1896).

committees within the Court to which cases were parceled out, even for determination of whether they would be heard, but that every Justice considered and passed upon every case presented to the Court. Sixty years later, his grandson, the present Justice John M. Harlan, was making the same explanation to members of the contemporary bar who had indicated a similar misconception.[2] Justice William J. Brennan, Jr., in the speech reprinted in this collection,[3] defends the Court's use of "social science data" in reaching its decisions, partly in answer to Southern critics of the desegregation rulings. Justice Felix Frankfurter's noted address, "The Supreme Court in the Mirror of the Justices" [4] demolishes the argument advanced by some influential journalists and Congressmen in the late 1940's that all Justices should have judicial experience before they are appointed.

Second, while the speeches of the Justices are defensive of the Establishment, they air clearly the fundamental differences within the Court as to basic judicial philosophy and specific topics of constitutional law. Justice Hugo Black's address in 1960, "The Bill of Rights" [5] (reprinted here), carries onto the speaker's rostrum his disagreement with the so-called "Frankfurter-Harlan" approach to civil-liberty issues. Justice Robert H. Jackson closed his life in the midst of writing a set of three lectures[6] (two of which appear here), in which he gave his mature speculations about the entire range of questions concerning judicial review in a democratic system; his strictures against the "cult of libertarian activists" in the Court left little to the imagination as to whom or what he meant. Thus the public statements of the Justices carry on the dialogue from the Conference Room and the opinions, and sometimes the freedom from fact-situations, precedents, and the parties of a specific case lead a Justice to express in revealing fashion the assumptions which underlie and shape his position.

Third, the Justices, by tradition, leak out informative bits of fact in their speeches and memoirs. Justice Felix Frankfurter, for

[2] "Some Aspects of Handling a Case in the United States Supreme Court," speech at the Annual Dinner of the New York State Bar Association, New York City, January 26, 1957.

[3] "Law and the Social Sciences," 24 *Vital Speeches* 143 (1957).

[4] 105 *University of Pennsylvania Law Review* 781 (1957).

[5] 35 *New York University Law Review* 865 (1960).

[6] *The Supreme Court in the American System of Government.* Cambridge, Mass., Harvard Univ., 1955.

example, disclosed in 1955, at a memorial lecture,[7] a private mem-
orandum given to Frankfurter by the late Justice Owen D. Roberts;
this showed that Roberts had *not* made the so-called "switch in
time which saved nine" in the minimum-wage cases of 1936-1937.
In his memoir, *All In One Lifetime*,[8] former Justice James F.
Byrnes describes the intra-Court consideration of several leading
cases decided during his year on the Court in 1941, including
an account of how an opinion which began as a dissent became
the majority statement.

In addition to the factual disclosures, the Justices have used
the broad opportunities of speeches and essays to reflect on the
dilemmas of judging. Justice Frankfurter has questioned whether
the members of the judiciary have really said much of note about
their own area. Speaking to the American Philosophical Society
in 1954,[9] Justice Frankfurter speculated:

Those who know tell me that the most illuminating light on
painting has been furnished by painters, and that the deepest
revelations on the writing of poetry have come from poets. It is
not so with the business of judging. The power of searching
analysis of what it is that they are doing seems rarely to be
possessed by judges, either because they are lacking in the art of
critical exposition, or because they are inhibited from practicing
it. The fact is that pitifully little of significance has been contributed by judges regarding the nature of their endeavor.

If Justice Frankfurter means that no judge has yet produced a
masterpiece of introspective analysis as to wise judging in constitutional cases, he is certainly correct. But if the standard is a
portrayal of how particular Justices and their ideological confreres
approach their task, what they consider relevant to decision, and
how they strike the four or five major balances of competing values
which every sensitive Justice consciously makes—if these are the
goals of discussion, then more than a few notable contributions can
be cited. After his always graceful warnings about the proprieties
which imprison Justices giving public addresses, Justice Brennan has

[7] "Mr. Justice Roberts," 104 *University of Pennsylvania Law Review* 311
(1955).
[8] New York, N. Y., Harpers, 1958.
[9] "Some Observations on the Nature of the Judicial Process of Supreme Court
Litigation," 98 *Proceedings of the American Philosophical Society* 233 (1954).

discussed judicial review and the difference between a state court judge's role and that of a Supreme Court Justice in a revealing fashion. Justice Frankfurter himself, in at least a dozen luminous essays on judicial behavior, has provided an abundance of superb commentary. Many of the speeches of Justices William O. Douglas and Robert H. Jackson, to mention only two others, fall into this category. All of these have the special quality of revealing "the view from inside." They show the collegial tug of war, the sense of being riveted to the seat of decision when events collide and perspective is not available, the awareness that in a nation worshiping pragmatism from its elected leaders, the Supreme Court serves as Political Theorist to a people.

Finally, the out-of-court statements of the Justices take on a special significance as we begin the 1960's. Before the 1940's, much of the national debate over the Court was in the form of proposals from the liberal community to cut the power of the Court and limit the discretion of the Justices. Since the early 1950's, the liberal community has aligned itself staunchly with the Court because of its civil-liberty, civil-rights, and business-regulation opinions. The business community, once the Court's unswerving and basic ally, has become neutralist, at best, toward its former partner-in-conservatism. Southerners, law-enforcement officers, and the internal-security zealots have declared war on the Court since the flow of rulings rejecting their positions, especially in the 1954-1959 period. In this unique setting of group alignments, the Justices, balanced between New- Fair-Deal appointees and the essentially "New Republican" designees of President Eisenhower, have had to re-define the role of the Court in relation to popular, majority-will measures. Where once the issues were property matters, they are now primarily liberty and equality issues. Thus, while much of the traditional apologetic for judicial review retains its meaning, the defense and the explanations must be recast to explain the new situation, to carry along the new liberal allies, and to pacify the older, estranged groups if possible. Therefore, what the Justices have said in the late 1950's and in 1960 is particularly significant, since this indicates how far the Justices felt it necessary to enunciate and defend their new institutional position between 1956 and 1960.

The desirability of sampling this present mood of the Justices, in a short volume for the college student and the general reader, has dictated the exclusion of two types of judicial commentary which otherwise would have been included: speeches by Justices before 1948, and the Justices' biographical estimates of former colleagues and predecessors. What this anthology offers, therefore, is a *contemporary* view from inside.

In Part One, "Justice at Work," five Justices discuss aspects of what might be called the "institutional filter of decision" in the Supreme Court: the Justices' image of the place of the Court in the American scheme of government; their understanding of their roles as individuals within the Court itself; the formal rules by which judicial business is conducted; and the informal practices or judicial folkways which affect the way in which the rules are applied. For those who need reminding, the selections indicate that debate over roles and rules starts at the Court's own conference table.

Part Two, "Court, Congress and the States," contains a discussion by three Justices of the Court's relations with Congress: Justices Douglas and Frankfurter probe the problems of statesmanship and craftsmanship involved in construing Congressional statutes; Justice Roberts submits a sturdy brief in behalf of a constitutional amendment to protect the Court from external and internal dangers; his discussion of the need to forestall hostile Congressional legislation cutting the Court's appellate jurisdiction came only a few years before the "court-curb" debates of 1957-59. The last selection in this Part, by Justice Brennan, was a speech defending the Court's duty to umpire the federal system, and it may not have been wholly accidental that the address coincided with condemnations of the Court's trend of decision in federal-state relations cases by the Chief Justices of the state supreme courts and the state Attorneys-General.

Part Three, "Precedent, Segregation, and 'The Law,'" opens with a sharp attack upon the Court for its 1954 decision holding segregated public schools to be unconstitutional. The author, former Justice James F. Byrnes, had he still been a member of the Court, would very likely have written almost the same words in a dissenting opinion. No present member of the Court has spoken publicly in defense of the de-segregation rulings. However, Justice Douglas' essay on *stare decisis* and Justice Brennan's defense of utilization of social science findings by "the law" indicate the contrary attitudes to that of former Justice Byrnes which underlay the de-segregation doctrines.

Part Four, "Liberty and Judicial Review," is a debate between two eloquent spokesmen for alternative judicial positions on court review in civil liberty cases. The late Justice Jackson surrounded his discussion with a full-dress consideration of the Court's role in all of the central problems of judicial review, while Mr. Justice Black limited his essay largely to the civil liberty field. Set alongside each other, though, the two arguments air thoroughly the basic issues involved in this controversy.

Now, the time for comments from outside is over. Let the views from inside begin.

PART ONE

Justice at Work

"The Supreme Court is a tribunal of limited jurisdiction, narrow processes, and small capacity for handling mass litigation; it has no force to coerce obedience, and is subject to being stripped of jurisdiction or smothered with additional Justices any time such a disposition exists and is supported strongly enough by public opinion. I think the Court can never quite escape consciousness of its own infirmities, a psychology which may explain its apparent yielding to expediency. . . ."

Mr. Justice Jackson

"It is asked with sophomoric brightness, does a man cease to be himself when he becomes a Justice? Does he change his character by putting on a gown? No, he does not change his character. He brings his whole experience, his training, his outlook, his social, intellectual and moral environment with him when he takes a seat on the Supreme Bench. But a judge worth his salt is in the grip of his function. . . . To assume that a lawyer who becomes a judge takes on the bench merely his views on social or economic questions leaves out of account his rooted notions regarding the scope and limits of a judge's authority. . . ."

Mr. Justice Frankfurter

"When one starts to write an opinion for the Supreme Court of the United States he learns the full meaning of the statement of Rufus Choate that 'one cannot drop the Greek alphabet to the ground and pick up the Iliad'."

Mr. Justice Clark

"When judges do not agree, it is a sign that they are dealing with problems on which society itself is divided. . . . The judiciary is a coordinate branch of government, bearing great responsibilities. The judge that writes his own predilections into the law in disregard of constitutional principles or the legislative or executive edicts that he interprets is not worthy of the great traditions of the bench. The judge that quavers or retreats before an impending crisis of the day and finds haven in dialectics or weasel words or surrenders his own conviction for a passing expediency is likewise not born for the woolsack. . . ."

Mr. Justice Douglas

ROBERT H. JACKSON
ASSOCIATE JUSTICE, 1941-1954

The Supreme Court as a Unit of Government[*]

. . . No sound assessment of our Supreme Court can treat it as an isolated, self-sustaining, or self-sufficient institution. It is a unit of a complex, interdependent scheme of government from which it cannot be severed. Nor can it be regarded merely as another law court. The Court's place in the combination was determined by principles drawn from a philosophy broader than mere law.

Our foundations were quarried not only from the legal ideas but also from the political, social, philosophical, scientific, and theological learnings of the eighteenth century, "the silver age of the Renaissance." All these were dominated by a belief in "the laws of nature and of nature's God." Faith in a "higher law," which had achieved a venerable place in the history of ideas through the speculations of jurists, monks, and scholars, burst forth toward the end of the eighteenth century into a fanatical creed that took over French and American liberal thinking and led in each case to a violent revolution.

Our judicial, executive, and legislative branches all were grounded in a belief that they were bound by the authority of a clear and universally acceptable natural law, revealed by man's reason and always and everywhere the same. Its fundamentals were proclaimed self-evident truths, as indisputable as the axioms of geometry, which needed only to be declared to be acknowl-

* Reprinted by permission of the publishers from Robert H. Jackson, *The Supreme Court in the American System of Government.* Cambridge, Mass., Harvard University Press, pp. 2-27. Copyright 1955 by William Eldred Jackson and G. Gowdoin Craighill, Jr., Executors. Footnotes omitted.

edged as right and just by the opinion of mankind. These truths of natural law to that age stood as the ultimate sanction of liberty and justice, equality and toleration. The whole constitutional philosophy of the time was based on a system of values in which the highest was the freedom of the individual from interference by officialdom—the rights of man. To supplement this natural order, little man-made government was thought to be needed, and the less the better.

To make certain that these natural rights should have some man-made sanctions, the forefathers added ten Amendments to the original instrument, translating their version of the rights of man into legal limitations on the new government. They did not stop, as the French did, at reciting these in a preamble to the Constitution, where they served as an admonition only to a parliament that was all-powerful because there could be no judicial review of its legislation. On the contrary, the forefathers established a Bill of Rights which conferred as a matter of law, enforceable in court, certain immunities and rights upon citizens which correspondingly limited the power of the majority duly expressed through governmental action. The whole spirit of this was to make secure the liberties which were what men in that age most wanted of the law. I find little indication that they foresaw a technique by which those liberties might be used to destroy themselves by immunizing a movement of a minority to impose upon the country an incompatible scheme of values which did not include political and civil liberties. The resort to that technique in this country, however fruitless, contemporaneously with the collapse or capture of free governments abroad, has stirred American anxieties deeply.

What we face today on an intellectual level is the climax of a long-gathering conflict between opposite poles of thought. Our traditional high valuation of individual liberty conflicts with the totalitarians' higher valuation of group interest within the state. Communism, Naziism, and Fascism have each made phenomenally successful drives to capture the minds and loyalties of numerous and aspiring peoples for this philosophy so antithetic to our own.

It is not possible to detail all of the American trends which, rightly or wrongly, have cooled the zeal of our own people for the principles on which our government was founded. Our own indifference, deviations, and dissatisfactions are largely the reason why our principles make so anemic and sterile an appearance in the world-wide struggle for the minds of men. The majestic phrases of the forefathers, even as they were penned, were being drained of their fervor. Men were already ceasing to ask "What must I do to be saved?" and were asking "What can I do to become rich, powerful, and honored?"

As men's minds turned more to material advancement, and the industrial revolution introduced new means both to satisfy and to stimulate the acquisitive instincts, a riotous competition was touched off for the spoils of the world and for exploitation of working and consuming masses. The inherently obscure and oracular character of natural law led courts to respond to the pressure of the times by making it a sanction for *laissez faire;* and skeptics, historians, and jurists joined in discrediting it. The nineteenth century closed with Americans repeating the phrases of the Declaration of Independence about the laws of nature and of nature's God, but the real attitude was that attributed by Knickerbocker to the Connecticut Yankees, who resolved to be governed by the laws of God—until they found time to make better ones. The so-called positivists took over, and any command that some authority had physical power to enforce became law. Since the Nürnberg post-mortem on the Hitler regime, few will believe that these positivist doctrines are weapons in the struggle to preserve liberty.

Meanwhile, Marx and Engels, two strangers to the actual workings of our American system, had formulated the revolutionary scheme of values which under new leadership is now our worldwide rival. Their doctrine teaches that there is no such thing as natural law or impartial justice, that the law is and should be the weapon of the class in power and administered in its interests, that law rests on the authority of force and not on any inherent rightfulness, that the object of its protection is the dominant group rather than the individual, and that it should not be administered by neutral judges but by class-conscious and class-serving judges. The Communists reject our claims to liberty as abstract intellectualism, if not hypocrisy, and claim that our free government is a sham to conceal economic exploitation of the most numerous class—the proletariat—which should be aroused to support the Communists in containment of our system and its eventual overthrow.

Our forefathers' conception of a liberal legal order had been the dynamic ideology of most of the nineteenth century. But the twentieth century has seen the depressed masses in nearly all backward countries abandon it as their hope and turn to a militant communism radiating from the Soviet Union, which Clement Attlee once described as merely "an inverted czardom." It dawns upon us that we are in an age of almost worldwide reaction, indeed, of counterrevolution, against the teachings and philosophy of our American Revolution and our Constitution. Revolutions in our time, whether by Communists, Fascists, or Nazis, have not pretended to overthrow or moderate the power of the state over the individual, but, instead, have each aspired to concentrate in the state a more absolute power over every activity of life and leave nothing but tatters of the "rights of man." Paradoxical as it may seem, we are in an age of rebellion against liberty. The rise of this new doctrine has brought about one of the most bloody and cruel half-centuries in the annals of mankind, one which has put to death or enslaved more people solely because of racial or national origin and political or economic views or status than ever before in history. This violence that civilization has experienced was not a repetition of physical overthrow from barbarians without. Civilization is still threatened by forces generated within and perhaps by itself.

Fortunately, up to now America has escaped any catastrophic impact from this turn of events. With few exceptions these revolutionary ideas have made their appeal to those we have long deemed backward peoples. The old and the new did not confront each other in our country with such provocative contrasts as in some other lands. We entered each of the great wars late, and while our collective resources were strained, they were not exhausted. Individual living standards were depressed, but not to the point of misery. It is true that we have suffered some intellectual demoralization, which has proceeded far—to the point where speculative freedom is regarded as the equivalent of revolutionary action. But intolerance, suspicion, and hatred still resort only to verbal and legalistic weapons and have not sunk to a regime of physical violence.

Nevertheless, it would have been too much to expect that the American mind would be wholly free from the influence of counterrevolutionary currents of thought which have captivated other peoples or that each of the ideologies which have divided the rest of the world would not find some followers and sympathizers here. Unfortunately, liberal-minded citizens have sometimes become entangled with Communist teachings, while many conservative citizens have reacted by favoring some form of "strong" government controlled by themselves—the reaction which elsewhere brought about Naziism and Fascism. It is time that we reëxamine the strength and defects of our own system, for we cannot longer regard the world-wide revolt against its animating principles as a local or passing flash in the pan. The fact is that we face a rival, secularized system of faith and order spread with a religious fervor not witnessed since the tides of Islamic fanaticism receded. We are brought into sudden and bitter competition with a whole new concept of the nature and use of social and political organization, a rivalry for which we are prepared intellectually even less than militarily.

Against this background a study of the Supreme Court can hardly fail to be instructive. First, the Court is distinctly a product of our founders' philosophy in some of its most important functions, and no counterpart has existed or can exist in those areas of the world which have traded individual liberty for totalitarianism. Second, this Court, structurally and functionally, has survived an attempt by President Roosevelt to reorganize it so as to eliminate a "judicial activism" which was impairing a program supported by large popular majorities. Third, soon thereafter the Court passed, by the process of mortality and replacement, almost entirely into the hands of those who were its former critics, and they have now had over a decade of its control. Fourth, not one of the basic power conflicts which precipitated the Roosevelt struggle against the judiciary has been eliminated or settled, and the old conflict between the branches of the Government remains, ready to break out again whenever the provocation becomes sufficient.

We ought first to inquire what kind of institution the Supreme Court really is, the degree of its independence, the nature of its power, and the limitations on its capacity and effectiveness. . . .

The Supreme Court of the United States was created in a

different manner from most high courts. In Europe, most judiciaries evolved as subordinates to the King, who delegated to them some of his functions. For example, while the English judges have developed a remarkably independent status, they still retain the formal status of Crown servants. But here, the Supreme Court and the other branches of the Federal Government came into existence at the same time and by the same act of creation. "We the People of the United States" deemed an independent Court equally as essential as a Congress or an Executive, especially, I suppose, to "establish Justice, insure domestic Tranquility," and to "secure the Blessings of Liberty to ourselves and to our Posterity." The status of the Court as a unit of the Government, not as an institution subordinate to it, no doubt has given it prestige, for the people do not regard the Justices as employees of the Government of the day or as civil servants, as in continental Europe. Also, federal judges enjoy two bulwarks of independence —life tenure (except for impeachable misbehavior) and irreducible salaries (except by taxation and inflation).

Nonetheless, the Constitution-makers left the Court in vital respects a dependent body. The political branches nominate and confirm the Justices, a control of the Court's composition which results in a somewhat lagging political influence over its trend of decision, and any party that prevails in the Federal Government through several presidential terms will gradually tend to impress its political philosophy on the Court. The political branches also from time to time may alter the number of Justices, and that power was used to influence the course of decision several times before it was again proposed by President Roosevelt.

The Court also is dependent on the political branches for its powers in other vital respects. Its only irrevocable jurisdiction is original, and that reaches only cases affecting Ambassadors, public Ministers, or Consuls, or cases in which a state is a party. In all other cases it has appellate jurisdiction, but "with such exceptions and under such regulations as Congress shall make." One Congress, fearing a decision unfavorable to its post-Civil War enactments, ousted the Court of jurisdiction in a case that had already been argued, and the Court submitted. The Court also is dependent upon the political branches for the execution of its mandates, for it has no physical force at its command. The story is traditional that President Jackson once withheld enforcement, saying, "John Marshall has made his decision:—*now let him enforce it!*" Also, the Court, of course, depends upon Congress for the appropriation of funds with which to operate. These all add up to a fairly formidable political power over the Supreme Court, if there were a disposition to exert it.

But perhaps the most significant and least comprehended limitation upon the judicial power is that this power extends only to cases and controversies. We know that this restriction was deliberate, for it was proposed in the Convention that the Supreme Court be made part of a Council of Revision with a kind of veto power, and this was rejected.

The result of the limitation is that the Court's only power is to decide lawsuits between adversary litigants with real interests at stake, and its only method of proceeding is by the conventional judicial, as distinguished from legislative or administrative, process. This precludes the rendering of advisory opinions even at the request of the nation's President and every form of pronouncement on abstract, contingent, or hypothetical issues. It prevents acceptance for judicial settlement of issues in which the interests and questions involved are political in character. It also precludes imposition on federal constitutional courts of nonjudicial duties. Recent trends to empower judges to grant or deny wire-tapping rights to a prosecutor or to approve a waiver of prosecution in order to force a witness to give self-incriminating testimony raise interesting and dubious questions. A federal court can perform but one function—that of deciding litigations—and can proceed in no manner except by the judicial process.

In his pioneering studies, Judge Cardozo demonstrated that this is not the rigid and inflexible process some of our ancestors thought it to be. But its inherent methods make it unfit for solving some kinds of problems which elements of our society have from time to time expected the Supreme Court to settle.

While the President or the Congress can take up any subject at any time, a court in our Anglo-American system is a substantially passive instrument, to be moved only by the initiative of litigants. The Supreme Court cannot take most cases until at least one and generally two courts below have heard and decided them, which, with the present congestion of calendars, may be very long indeed. Also, as an appellate court, it properly can act only on the state of facts revealed by the record made in the court below, supplemented sometimes by general information of which it may take judicial notice. Hence a claim of right may be prejudiced by the incompetence, carelessness, or collusion of attorneys, as where they fail to make an adequate record to support the question sought to be raised. The decision of a case also may depend on its peculiarities of fact, for it is still true that hard cases make bad law. And when it is all over, the judicial decree, however broadly worded, actually binds, in most instances, only the parties to the case. As to others, it is merely a weather vane showing which way the judicial wind is blowing—a precedent that the Court in a similar case is likely to follow. Its real weight in subsequent cases, however, will depend on many factors, such as the quality of the prevailing opinion, the strength of any dissent, the acceptance or criticism by the profession, and the experience in application of the rule. Thus, the process of the courts is adapted to the intensive examination of particular legal grievances.

No conclusion as to what can be expected of the Court is valid which overlooks the measure of its incapacity to entertain and decide cases under its traditional working methods. With few exceptions, Congress has found it necessary to make review in the Supreme Court not the right of a litigant but a discretionary matter with the Court itself, in order to keep the volume of its business within its capacity. Last term, review was sought by appeal and certiorari in 1,452 cases, only 119 of which were allowed. It is not necessary to detail the considerations which move the Court to grant review beyond saying that the grant is not intended merely to give a litigant another chance, nor does it depend on the dollars involved or the private interests affected, but upon the importance of the case to a uniform and just system of federal law.

The routine during the Court term has been to hear arguments the first five days of each two weeks, followed by two weeks of recess for the writing of opinions and the study of the appeals and certiorari petitions, which must be disposed of periodically. The time allowed for each side to argue its case is normally one hour, and, in cases where the question seems not complex, it is half of that. In the early days of the Supreme Court, the volume of work permitted argument to extend over several days, as it still does in the House of Lords. Many cases argued before us today in two hours have taken days, weeks, and even months in the trial court or administrative body.

What really matters to the lawyer and the law is what happens between the argument and the decision. On each Saturday following argument or preceding a decision Monday, the Court holds its only regularly scheduled conference. It begins at 11 a.m. and rarely ends before 5:30 p.m. With a half-hour for lunch, this gives about 360 minutes in which to complete final consideration of forthcoming opinions, the noting of probable jurisdiction of appeals, the disposition of petitions for certiorari, petitions for rehearing and miscellaneous matters, and the decision of argued cases. The largest conference list during the October 1953 term contained 145 items, the shortest 24, the average 70. A little computation will show that the average list would permit, at the average conference, an average of five minutes of deliberation per item, or about 33 seconds of discussion per item by each of the nine Justices, assuming, of course, that each is an average Justice who does the average amount of talking.

All that saves the Court from being hopelessly bogged down is that many of these items are so frivolous on mere inspection that no one finds them worthy of discussion, and they are disposed of by unanimous consent. Even eliminating these, the time devoted at conference to argued cases is inadequate for detailed deliberation and results, more or less, in a canvass of impressions with the understanding that a vote on any case is tentative and on later consideration may be changed. And not infrequently the detailed study required to write an opinion, or the persuasiveness of an opinion or dissent, will lead to a change of a vote or even to a change of result. If there is further conferring, it is unofficial, usually between two or more Justices of like mind in the particular case.

The pressure of time may induce an attitude that discussion in conference is futile and thereby contributes to the multiplicity of individual opinions. It is often easier to write out one's own view than for nine men in such short time to explore their doubts and difficulties together, or to reach a reconciliation of viewpoints. The fact is that the Court functions less as one deliberative body than as nine, each Justice working largely in isolation except as he chooses to seek consultation with others. These working methods tend to cultivate a highly individualistic rather than a group viewpoint.

The individual study which any case receives before or after argument is the affair of each Justice. All receive the printed briefs and record, in some cases short, in others running to a great many volumes. Some records take five feet of shelf space. It is easily demonstrated that no Justice possibly could read more than a fraction of the printed matter filed with the Court each year. Nor is it necessary that he should. But as to his individual labors, with this mountain of papers, each Justice is the keeper of his own conscience.

In argued cases, conferences are followed by the preparation and circulation of opinions by Justices designated by the Chief Justice when he is with the prevailing view and, if not, by the senior Associate who is. But any Justice is free to write as he will, and there may be one or more opinions concurring in the result but reaching it by different reasons, and there may be a dissenting opinion or opinions. This occasions complaint by laymen and the bar that they are required to piece all these contributions together in order to make out where the Supreme Court really stands as an institution.

All of this is at odds with the practice of most courts of continental Europe, which make it a rule to announce the decision in one statement only and to issue no dissents or concurrences. Moreover, their work is institutionalized and depersonalized. The court's opinion bears the name of no author. Like our *per curiam* opinion, it may be the work of any member or of several in collaboration. This anonymity diminishes any temptation to exploit differences within the court, but it may also diminish the incentive for hard work on opinions. In any event, I am sure that not only Anglo-American tradition but judicial and professional opinion favors the identification of writers and the full disclosure of important differences within the Court. Mr. Jefferson would have required each Justice to write his reasons in every case, as proof that he gave it consideration and did not merely follow a leader.

The dissenting opinion strives to undermine the Court's reasoning and discredit its result. At its best, the dissent, as Mr. Hughes said, is "an appeal to the brooding spirit of the law, to the intelligence of a future day. . . ." But Judge Cardozo has written:

". . . Comparatively speaking at least, the dissenter is irresponsible. The spokesman of the court is cautious, timid, fearful of the vivid word, the heightened phrase. He dreams of an unworthy brood of scions, the spawn of careless *dicta*, disowned by the *ratio decidendi*, to which all legitimate offspring must be able to trace their lineage. The result is to cramp and paralyze. One fears to say anything when the peril of misunderstanding puts a warning finger to the lips. Not so, however, the dissenter. . . . For the moment, he is the gladiator making a last stand against the lions. The poor man must be forgiven a freedom of expression, tinged at rare moments with a touch of bitterness, which magnanimity as well as caution would reject for one triumphant."

Dissent has a popular appeal, for it is an underdog judge pleading for an underdog litigant. Of course, one party or the other must always be underdog in a lawsuit, the purpose of which really is to determine which one it shall be. But the tradition of great dissents built around such names as Holmes, Brandeis, Cardozo, and Stone is not due to the frequency or multiplicity of their dissents, but to their quality and the importance of the few cases in which they carried their disagreement beyond the conference table. Also, quite contrary to the popular notion, relatively few of all the dissents recorded in the Supreme Court have later become law, although some of these are of great importance.

There has been much undiscriminating eulogy of dissenting opinions. It is said they clarify the issues. Often they do the exact opposite. The technique of the dissenter often is to exaggerate the holding of the Court beyond the meaning of the majority and then to blast away at the excess. So the poor lawyer with a similar case does not know whether the majority opinion meant what it seemed to say or what the minority said it meant. Then, too, dissenters frequently force the majority to take positions more extreme than was originally intended. The classic example is the *Dred Scott Case*, in which Chief Justice Taney's extreme statements were absent in his original draft and were inserted only after Mr. Justice McLean, then a more than passive candidate for the presidency, raised the issue in dissent.

The *right of dissent* is a valuable one. Wisely used on well-chosen occasions, it has been of great service to the profession and to the law. But there is nothing good, for either the Court or the dissenter, in dissenting per se. Each dissenting opinion is a confession of failure to convince the writer's colleagues, and the true test of a judge is his influence in leading, not in opposing, his court.

If the Supreme Court were any kind of institution except a court, it would be easy to suggest methods by which it could dispose of an increased volume of work. The objection to most such proposals is that they are incompatible with the personal and individual responsibility inherent in judicial office.

It has been suggested that a small committee of the Court could pass on certiorari applications. Some lawyers believe that this is done. That is not true. The Supreme Court does not function on any case by committee. Every qualified Justice acts on every petition expressly or by acquiescence.

It is often suggested that the Court could create a staff of assistants like those of administrative tribunals to take much of the drudgery of judicial work from the Justices. In fact, a suspicion has grown at the bar that the law clerks already constitute a kind of junior court which decides the fate of certiorari petitions. This idea of the law clerks' influence gave rise to a lawyer's waggish statement that the Senate no longer need bother about confirmation of Justices but ought to confirm the appointment of law clerks. Twice during the last term I was asked by prominent lawyers, once by letter and once orally, how they could get their petitions for certiorari past law clerks and to the consideration of the Justices themselves. The answer is that every petition is on the conference list, and its fate is decided by the vote or agreement without formal vote of every Justice who does not disqualify himself.

The extent and methods of utilizing law clerks' services naturally differ with the individual Justices. The law clerks regard themselves and are regarded not as aides to the court, but as aides to the particular Justice who selects them. What a Justice delegates to his clerk will depend on the Justice's temperament and experience, but it is he who is responsible for his contribution to the Court's work. For myself, I believe that a court is one place where counsel should confront and address the very men who are to decide his case. I do not think judging can be a staff job, and I deplore whatever tendency there may be in the courts to make it such.

There have been suggestions that an increased work capacity could be obtained by enlarging the Court, which might then sit in sections or chambers as do some administrative bodies in this country and many courts abroad. The French Cour de Cassation and the Soviet Supreme Court both consist of sixty to seventy members who function, in fact, as several courts, each dealing with a specialized type of litigation; as, for example, commercial cases, other civil cases, criminal cases, military appeals, cases involving officials of the government, and admiralty cases. But our Constitution vests the judicial power in only "one supreme Court," and it has been the view of high authority that this precludes the Court from being split into chambers or sections; also, there has never been either political or professional sentiment in this country in favor of such a Supreme Court, and it would face very practical difficulties even if it were permissible under the Constitution.

The only way found practicable or acceptable in this country for keeping the volume of cases within the capacity of a court of last resort is to allow the intermediate courts of appeal finally to settle all cases that are of consequence only to parties. This reserves to the court of last resort only questions on which lower courts are in conflict or those of general importance to the law.

From what I have said it might almost be assumed that the Supreme Court could be ignored in the power equation of the American Government. But in living history this institution has profoundly influenced, for better or for worse, the course of the nation. Not only has it been the center of bitter debate itself, but its decisions have played some part in nearly every great political issue that has vexed our people.

What authority does the Court possess which generates this influence? The answer is its power to hold unconstitutional and judicially unenforceable an act of the President, of Congress, or of a constituent state of the Federation. That power is not expressly granted or hinted at in the Article defining judicial power, but rests on logical implication. It is an incident of jurisdiction to determine what really is the law governing a particular case or controversy. In the hierarchy of legal values, if the higher law of the Constitution prohibits what the lower law of the legislature attempts, the latter is a nullity; otherwise, the Constitution would exist only at the option of Congress. Thus it comes about that in

a private litigation the Court may decide a question of power
that will be of great moment to the nation or to a state.

The assertion of this power over the enactments of the states
met with strong resistance, and its application to laws of Congress
provoked bitter and persistent opposition. It is needless to trace
the evolution of the power as now exercised. The Rooseveltian
struggle with the Court did not impair the power, which is as posi-
tively asserted today as in pre-Roosevelt days. But neither did that
struggle end the controversy over the proper use of the power, a
controversy which lies just beneath the surface and is likely to
break forth from time to time as long as the Republic shall last.

Public opinion, however, seems always to sustain the power of
the Court, even against attack by popular executives and even
though the public more than once has repudiated particular decisions. It is inescapable in our form of government that authority
exists somewhere to interpret an instrument which sets up our
whole structure and defines the powers of the Federal Government in about 4,000 words, to which a century and a half have
added only about half as many amendatory words. The people
have seemed to feel that the Supreme Court, whatever its defects,
is still the most detached, dispassionate, and trustworthy cus-
todian that our system affords for the translation of abstract into
concrete constitutional commands.

The Constitution has gone through several cycles of interpretation, each of which is related to the political and economic
condition of the period. Federal powers were consolidated and
invigorated under Marshall. A reaction marked by conflict over
the very nature and binding force of the compact embittered the
time of Taney. There followed a period when attention turned
to nationalism and to railroad building and industrial growth
stimulated by a long period of almost uninterrupted peace. That
came to an end in 1914, and we entered the period of international violence which now burdens and vexes us and puts our
internal liberties under new strains.

That the Supreme Court, in some instances, can interpose
judicial authority between political forces and those whose liberty
they would override is a great distinction from those governments abroad which have been subverted by dictatorship. But I
have tried to point out that while our judiciary is an effective
instrument for applying to the case of an individual the just

laws enacted by representatives of a freedom-respecting society, it has grave jurisdictional, procedural, and political shortcomings. These counsel against leaving the protection of liberty wholly to the judiciary, while heedlessly allowing the elected branches of the Government to be constituted without regard to their members' attitudes toward liberty.

Let us take the factor of delay. Since the Court may pronounce a judgment of unconstitutionality only in deciding a case or controversy, obviously it cannot take the initiative in checking what the Justices may know to be constitutional violations. It has no self-starting capacity and must await the action of some litigant so aggrieved as to have a justiciable case. Also, its pronouncement must await the decision in the lower courts. Often it is years after a statute is put on the books and begins to take effect before a decision on a constitutional question can be heard by the Supreme Court. The Smith Act of 1940 was held constitutional for the first time in 1951, and the Alien Registration Act, also of 1940, was passed on in 1952. The run of constitutional litigation, like that of all litigations, is slow and costly.

Such delays often mean that the damage is done before the remedy for invasion of civil liberties is available. For example: In 1951 the Court cast serious doubt upon the legality of the Attorney General's list of subversive organizations promulgated in 1947. But the list had long been widely circulated and accepted, and despite the Court's views it has never ceased to be used in the press, in the executive department, by and before congressional committees, and even in courts to prejudice individuals in their liberty, position, and good name.

Then, too, many of the most vital acts of government cannot be challenged at all by the case and controversy route, because the questions are political or involve the spending power, foreign affairs, or the war power. The Supreme Court is a tribunal of limited jurisdiction, narrow processes, and small capacity for handling mass litigation; it has no force to coerce obedience, and is subject to being stripped of jurisdiction or smothered with additional Justices any time such a disposition exists and is supported strongly enough by public opinion. I think the Court can never quite escape consciousness of its own infirmities, a psychology which may explain its apparent yielding to expediency, especially during war time.

If I may borrow a summation from my former self, I will re-peat to you the conclusion of a lecture to the lawyers of the Ministry of Justice of France, delivered at their invitation in April 1946, when they were in the throes of writing a new con-stitution for France. After discussing the judicial vis-à-vis the political power in our system, I said:

"Opinion, of course, will differ as to the advantages and dis-advantages of this constitutional and judicial system. The United States on the whole has been a prosperous country, with varied resources, making a favorable background for any experiment in government. Its inhabitants have not faced the strains that beset some less-favored nations. Even so, our history has not been free of sanguinary internal conflicts. It would not be realistic to contend that judicial power always has been used wisely. The Court has been sharply attacked by Presidents Jefferson, Jackson, Lincoln, and both Roosevelts. Yet no substantial sentiment exists for any curtailment of the Court's powers. Even President Roose-velt in the bitterest conflict with judicial power in our history suggested only change in the Court's composition, none in its constitutional prerogatives. The real strength of the position of the Court is probably in its indispensability to government under a written Constitution. It is difficult to see how the provisions of a 150-year-old written document can have much vitality if there is not some permanent institution to translate them into current commands and to see to their contemporary application. Courts will differ from time to time in the emphasis they will place on one or another of the Constitution's provisions, in part no doubt responsive to the atmosphere of the changes in public opinion. Interpretations will change from one generation to an-other, precedents will sometimes be overruled, innovations will be made that will not always be predictable. This always has been the history of the Supreme Court.

"The legal profession in all countries knows that there are only two real choices of government open to a people. It may be governed by law or it may be governed by the will of one or of a group of men. Law, as the expression of the ultimate will and wisdom of a people, has so far proven the safest guardian of liberty yet devised. I think our constitutional and judicial system has made a valuable and enduring contribution to the science of government under law. We commend it to your notice, not because we think it is perfect, but because it is an earnest effort to fulfill those aspirations for freedom and the general welfare which are a common heritage of your people and of mine."

FELIX FRANKFURTER

ASSOCIATE JUSTICE, 1939—

The Process of Judging
in the Supreme Court[*]

. . . I am advised by an arithmetically-minded scholar that the
Constitution of the United States is composed of some 6,000
words. Not every provision of that document that becomes controversial can come before the Supreme Court for adjudication.
The questions that are not meet for judicial determination have
elicited their own body of literature. A hint of the nature of such
questions is given by their fair characterization as an exercise of
judicial self-limitation. This area constitutes one very important
and very troublesome aspect of the Court's functioning—its duty
not to decide.

Putting to one side instances of this judicial self-restraint, de
Tocqueville showed his characteristic discernment when he wrote:
"Scarcely any political question arises in the United States that
is not resolved sooner or later into a judicial question." Those
provisions of the Constitution that do raise justiciable issues vary
in their incidence from time to time. The construction of all of
them, however, is related to the circumambient condition of our
Constitution—that our nation is a federalism. The most exacting problems that in recent years have come before the Court
have invoked two provisions expressed in a few undefined words—
the clause giving Congress power to regulate commerce among
the States and the Due Process Clauses of the Fifth and Fourteenth Amendments.

[*] Felix Frankfurter, "Some Observations on the Nature of the Judicial Process
of Supreme Court Litigation." 98 *Proceedings of the American Philosophical
Society* 233 (1954). Footnotes omitted. Reprinted by permission of Mr. Justice
Frankfurter and the publisher.

A federalism presupposes the distribution of governmental powers between national and local authority. Between these two authorities there is shared the power entirely possessed by a unitary state. In addition to the provisions of our Constitution making this distribution of authority between the two governments, there is also in the United States Constitution a withdrawal of power from both governments, or, at least, the exercise of governmental power is subject to limitations protective of the rights of the individual. Of the two types of constitutional provision calling for construction from case to case, the limitation in the interest of the individual presents the most delicate and most pervasive of all issues to come before the Court. For these cases involve no less a task than the accommodation by a court of the interest of an individual over against the interest of society.

Human society keeps changing. Needs emerge, first vaguely felt and unexpressed, imperceptibly gathering strength, steadily becoming more and more exigent, generating a force which, if left unheeded and denied response so as to satisfy the impulse behind it at least in part, may burst forth with an intensity that exacts more than reasonable satisfaction. Law as the response to these needs is not merely a system of logical deduction, though considerations of logic are far from irrelevant. Law presupposes sociological wisdom as well as logical unfolding. The nature of the interplay of the two has been admirably conveyed, if I may say so, by Professor Alfred North Whitehead:

It is the first step in sociological wisdom to recognize that the major advances in civilization are processes that all but wreck the societies in which they occur—like unto an arrow in the hand of a child. The art of free society consists first in the maintenance of the symbolic code; and secondly in fearlessness of revision, to secure that the code serves those purposes which satisfy an enlightened reason. Those societies which cannot combine reverence to their symbols with freedom of revision, must ultimately decay either from anarchy, or from the slow atrophy of a life stifled by useless shadows.

The Due Process Clauses of our Constitution are the vehicles for giving response by law to this felt need by allowing accommodations or modifications in the rules and standards that govern

the conduct of men. Obviously, therefore, due process as a concept is neither fixed nor finished.

The judgment of history on the inherently living and therefore changing applicability of due process was thus pronounced
by Mr. Justice Sutherland, one of the most traditionally minded
of judges:

Regulations, the wisdom, necessity and validity of which, as
applied to existing conditions, are so apparent that they are now
uniformly sustained, a century ago, or even half a century ago,
probably would have been rejected as arbitrary and oppressive.

A more expansive attempt at indicating the viable function of
the guarantee of due process was made in a recent opinion:

The requirement of "due process" is not a fair-weather or timid
assurance. It must be respected in periods of calm and in times of
trouble; it protects aliens as well as citizens. But "due process,"
unlike some legal rules, is not a technical conception with a fixed
content unrelated to time, place and circumstances. Expressing as
it does in its ultimate analysis respect enforced by law for that
feeling of just treatment which has been evolved through centuries of Anglo-American constitutional history and civilization,
"due process" cannot be imprisoned within the treacherous limits
of any formula. Representing a profound attitude of fairness between man and man, and more particularly between the individual and government, "due process" is compounded of
history, reason, the past course of decisions, and stout confidence in the strength of the democratic faith which we profess. Due process is not a mechanical instrument. It is not a
yardstick. It is a process. It is a delicate process of adjustment
inescapably involving the exercise of judgment by those whom
the Constitution entrusted with the unfolding of the process.

This conception of due process meets resistance from what has
been called our pigeon-holing minds which seek to rest unin-
quiringly on formulas—phrases which, as Holmes pointed out
long ago, "by their very felicity delay further analysis," and often
do so for a long time. This is, of course, a form of intellectual
indulgence, sometimes called the law of imitation. "Traditions
which no longer meet their original end" must be subjected to
the critique of history whereby we are enabled "to make up our

minds dispassionately whether the survival which we are enforcing answers any new purpose when it has ceased to answer the old."

Round phrases cannot give square answers. The law in the Court's keeping is not a system of logical abstractions. It is not enough to accept or reject, or even to qualify, so-called theories or principles. Before we can do that we must know their origin, development and association, "not excluding the special personal equations of their founders and promoters."

In giving expression through law to the demands of the time, the Court is concerned with how men feel—that is, with beliefs or assumptions which in one way or another enter into, when they do not underlie, juristic views and judgments. For instance, in passing upon claims by an Igorot tribesman to property, the Court recognized that the claims were based on long association, calling this "one of the profoundest factors in human thought"; in determining the responsibility of a corporation doing business outside of its chartering State, the Court moved out of the realm of fiction into that of business actualities by taking note of the fact that "[m]en's minds had become habituated to corporate activities which crossed state lines."

But a merely private judgment that the time has come for a shift of opinion regarding law does not justify such a shift. Departure from an old view, particularly one that has held unquestioned sway, "must be duly mindful of the necessary demands of continuity in a civilized society. A reversal of a long current of decisions can be justified only if rooted in the Constitution itself as an historic document designed for a developing nation." It makes an important difference, of course, if the validity of an old doctrine on which decisions were based was always in controversy and so did not embed deeply and widely in men's feelings justifiable reliance on the doctrine as part of the accepted outlook of society. What is most important, however, is that the Constitution of the United States, except in what might be called the skeleton or framework of our society—the anatomical as against the physiological aspects—"was designed for a developing nation." As to those features of our Constitution which raise the most frequent perplexities for decision by the Court, they were drawn in many particulars with purposeful vagueness so as to leave room for the unfolding but undisclosed future.

At this point one wishes there were time to document these generalizations with concrete instances which would help to define the problem and illustrate generalities from which the Court starts and differences of opinion which naturally enough arise in their application. Such documentation would expose divergencies by which common starting points lead to different destinations because of differences in emphasis and valuation in the process of reasoning. They would also shed some light on the interplay between language and thought. Differences in style eventually may embody differences of content, just as a sonnet may sometimes focus thought more trenchantly than a diffuse essay. It must suffice, however, merely to give intimations of the range of issues that are put to the test of the Due Process Clause, scant samples of the range and volume of cases in which due process is involved. Thus, the Court has been called upon to decide whether Michigan may forbid a woman from being a barmaid unless she be the wife or daughter of the owner, though, as we learn from Shakespeare, the alewife, sprightly and ribald, played a role in English social life. May Louisiana make pilotage on the Mississippi an hereditary calling? May New York release children from the public schools in collaboration with sectarian agencies so as to help shepherd children into classes for religious instruction? May Pennsylvania, in sections of the State with a polyglot population, require children to participate in flag-saluting exercises? Is it surprising that in the decisions on each of these questions, there was a sharp division on the Court?

This restriction of due process upon arbitrary exercise of governmental power is found only in our Constitution. The duty of judicially enforcing the indeterminate and undefinable restriction derived from "due process" places upon the Supreme Court a task with which no other comparable judicial body is charged. It is because of our experience that the framers of the other federal constitutions of the English-speaking world did not include such a provision. Neither the Supreme Court of Canada nor the High Court of Australia nor the Supreme Court of India is confronted with the almost intractable problems of judicial review which the Due Process Clauses in our Constitution engender. The Constitution of India, a document of brilliant and skillful draftsmanship, has perhaps the most elaborate provisions safeguarding what the statute abolishing the Star Chamber termed

"Liberties of the Subject," 16 Car. I, c. 10. But with full awareness of the course of our decisions, that ardently democratic
country decided not to have in its constitution the one provision
of our Bill of Rights, the Due Process Clause, which the Court
finds—certainly I do—the most perplexing. Fundamental principles of the kind for which shelter is often sought under the Due
Process Clause are set forth in the Constitution of India as
"Directive Principles of State Policy" which it is "the duty of
the State to apply . . . in making laws," but the provisions of
which "shall not be enforceable by any court."

The other major source of puzzling problems is the Commerce
Clause. With us the Commerce Clause is perhaps the most fruit-
ful and important means for asserting national authority against
the particularism of State policy. The role of the Court in striking
the balance between the respective spheres of federal and State
power was thus adumbrated by the Court:

The interpenetrations of modern society have not wiped out
state lines. It is not for us to make inroads upon our federal
system either by indifference to its maintenance or excessive regard for the unifying forces of modern technology. Scholastic
reasoning may prove that no activity is isolated within the boundaries of a single State, but that cannot justify absorption of legislative power by the United States over every activity. On the
other hand, the old admonition never becomes stale that this Court
is concerned with the bounds of legal power and not with the
bounds of wisdom in its exercise by Congress. When the conduct
of an enterprise affects commerce among the States is a matter of
practical judgment, not to be determined by abstract notions. The
exercise of this practical judgment the Constitution entrusts primarily and very largely to the Congress, subject to the latter's control by the electorate. Great power was thus given to the Congress: the power of legislation and thereby the power of passing
judgment upon the needs of a complex society. Strictly confined
though far-reaching power was given to this Court: that of determining whether the Congress has exceeded limits allowable in
reason for the judgment which it has exercised. To hold that
Congress could not deem the activities here in question to affect
what men of practical affairs would call commerce, and to deem
them related to such commerce merely by gossamer threads and
not by solid ties, would be to disrespect the judgment that is
open to men who have the constitutional power and responsibility
to legislate for the Nation.

The problems which the Commerce Clause raises as a result of the diffusion of power between a national government and its constituent parts are shared in variant forms by Canada, Australia and India. While the distribution of powers between each national government and its parts varies, leading at times to different legal results, the problems faced by the United States Supreme Court under the Commerce Clause are not different in kind, as are the problems of judicial review under the Due Process Clause, from those which come before the Supreme Court of Canada and the High Court of Australia.

Judicial judgment in these two classes of the most difficult cases must take deep account, if I may paraphrase Maitland, of the day before yesterday in order that yesterday may not paralyze today, and it must take account of what it decrees for today in order that today may not paralyze tomorrow.

A judge whose preoccupation is with such matters should be compounded of the faculties that are demanded of the historian and the philosopher and the prophet. The last demand upon him—to make some forecast of the consequences of his action— is perhaps the heaviest. To pierce the curtain of the future, to give shape and visage to mysteries still in the womb of time, is the gift of imagination. It requires poetic sensibilities with which judges are rarely endowed and which their education does not normally develop. These judges, you will infer, must have something of the creative artist in them; they must have antennae registering feeling and judgment beyond logical, let alone quantitative, proof.

At this point, Judge Learned Hand bears quoting:

I venture to believe that it is as important to a judge called upon to pass on a question of constitutional law, to have at least a bowing acquaintance with Acton and Maitland, with Thucydides, Gibbon and Carlyle, with Homer, Dante, Shakespeare and Milton, with Machiavelli, Montaigne and Rabelais, with Plato, Bacon, Hume and Kant, as with the books which have been specifically written on the subject. For in such matters everything turns upon the spirit in which he approaches the questions before him. The words he must construe are empty vessels into which he can pour nearly anything he will. Men do not gather figs of thistles, nor supply institutions from judges whose outlook is limited by parish or class. They must be aware that there are before them more than verbal problems; more than final solutions cast in generalizations of universal applicability. They must be aware of the changing social tensions in every society which make it an organism; which demand new schemata of adaptation; which will disrupt it, if rigidly confined.

The decisions in the cases that really give trouble rest on judgment, and judgment derives from the totality of a man's nature and experience. Such judgment will be exercised by two types of men, broadly speaking, but of course with varying emphasis—those who express their private views or revelations, deeming them, if not *vox dei*, at least *vox populi*; or those who feel strongly that they have no authority to promulgate law by their merely personal view and whose whole training and proved performance substantially insure that their conclusions reflect understanding of, and due regard for, law as the expression of the views and feelings that may fairly be deemed representative of the community as a continuing society.

Judges are men, not disembodied spirits. Of course a judge is not free from preferences or, if you will, biases. But he may deprive a bias of its meretricious authority by stripping it of the uncritical assumption that it is founded on compelling reason or the coercive power of a syllogism. He will be alert to detect that though a conclusion has a logical form it in fact represents a choice of competing considerations of policy, one of which for the time has won the day.

An acute historian recently concluded that those "who have any share of political power . . . usually obtain it because they are exceptionally able to emancipate their purposes from the control of their unformulated wishes and impressions." For judges, it is not merely a desirable capacity "to emancipate their purposes" from their private desire; it is their duty. It is a cynical belief in too many quarters, though I believe this cult of cynicism is receding, that it is at best a self-delusion for judges to profess to pursue disinterestedness. It is asked with sophomoric brightness, does a man cease to be himself when he becomes a Justice? Does he change his character by putting on a gown? No, he does not change his character. He brings his whole experience, his training, his outlook, his social, intellectual and moral environment with him when he takes a seat on the Supreme Bench. But a judge worth his salt is in the grip of his function. The intellectual habits of self-discipline which govern his mind are as much a part of him as the influence of the interest he may have represented at the bar, often much more so. For example, Mr. Justice Bradley was a "corporation lawyer" *par excellence* when he went on the Court. But his decisions on matters affecting corporate control in the years following the Civil War were strikingly free of bias in favor of corporate power.

To assume that a lawyer who becomes a judge takes on the bench merely his views on social or economic questions leaves out of account his rooted notions regarding the scope and limits of a judge's authority. The outlook of a lawyer fit to be a Justice regarding the role of a judge cuts across all his personal preferences for this or that social arrangement. The conviction behind what John Adams wrote in the provision of the Massachusetts Declaration of Rights regarding the place of the judiciary in our governmental scheme, and the considerations which led the Framers of the Constitution to give federal judges life tenure and other safeguards for their independence, have, I believe, dominated the outlook and therefore the action of the generality of men who have sat on the Supreme Court. Let me recall the Massachusetts Declaration:

It is essential to the preservation of the rights of every individual, his life, liberty, property, and character, that there be an impartial interpretation of the laws, and administration of justice. It is the right of every citizen to be tried by judges as free, impartial, and independent as the lot of humanity will admit. . . .

Need it be stated that true humility and its offspring, disinterestedness, are more indispensable for the work of the Supreme Court than for a judge's function on any other bench? These qualities alone will not assure another indispensable requisite. This is the capacity for self-searching. What Jacques Maritain said in another connection applies peculiarly to members of the Supreme Court. A Justice of that Court cannot adequately discharge his function "without passing through the door of the knowing, obscure as it may be, of his own subjective."

This is not to say that the application of this view of the judge's function—that he is there not to impose his private views upon society, that he is not to enforce personalized justice—assures unanimity of judgments. Inevitably there are bound to be fair differences of opinion. And it would be pretense to deny that in the self-righteous exercise of this role obscurantist and even unjustifiable decisions are sometimes rendered. Why should anyone be surprised at this? The very nature of the task makes some differences of view well nigh inevitable. The answers that the Supreme Court is required to give are based on questions and on data that preclude automatic or even undoubting answers. If the materials on which judicial judgments must be based could be fed into a machine so as to produce ineluctable answers, if such were the nature of the problems that come before the Supreme Court and such were the answers expected, we would have IBM machines doing the work instead of judges. [As Chief Justice Hughes once observed:]

How amazing it is that, in the midst of controversies on every conceivable subject, one should expect unanimity of opinion upon difficult legal questions! In the highest ranges of thought, in theology, philosophy and science, we find differences of view on the part of the most distinguished experts,—theologians, philosophers and scientists. The history of scholarship is a record of disagreements. And when we deal with questions relating to principles of law and their application, we do not suddenly rise into a stratosphere of icy certainty.

The core of the difficulty is that there is hardly a question of any real difficulty before the Court that does not entail more than one so-called principle. Anybody can decide a question if only a single principle is in controversy. Partisans and advocates often cast a question in that form, but the form is deceptive. In a famous passage Mr. Justice Holmes has exposed this misconception:

All rights tend to declare themselves absolute to their logical extreme. Yet all in fact are limited by the neighborhood of principles of policy which are other than those on which the particular right is founded, and which become strong enough to hold their own when a certain point is reached. . . . The boundary at which the conflicting interests balance cannot be determined by any general formula in advance, but points in the line, or helping to establish it, are fixed by decisions that this or that concrete case falls on the nearer or farther side.

This contest between conflicting principles is not limited to law. In a recent discussion of two books on the conflict between the claims of literary individualism and dogma, I came across this profound observation: ". . . But when, in any field of human observation, two truths appear in conflict it is wiser to assume that neither is exclusive, and that their contradiction, though it may be hard to bear, is part of the mystery of things." But judges cannot leave such contradiction between two conflicting "truths" as "part of the mystery of things." They have to adjudicate. If the conflict cannot be resolved, the task of the Court is to arrive at an accommodation of the contending claims. This is the core of the difficulties and misunderstandings about the judicial process. This, for any conscientious judge, is the agony of his duty.

TOM C. CLARK

Inside the Court[*]

. . . The lives of the members of the Supreme Court have been
described as being "of unremitting toil." As to this observation
Mr. Justice Hughes, later the Chief Justice, when told at his
induction ceremony that he was "entering upon a life of slavery,"
countered, "Yes, I know. I have experienced freedom and even it
has its illusions." I hasten to join in this view. . . .

All of you know what happens in our courtroom. Many of you
are familiar with the details of our schedule calling for argument
of counsel during a two week period, followed by two weeks of
recess. Argument sessions run from Monday through Thursday.
Each party at argument is allowed one hour, unless by reason of
the nature of the question the time is cut in half. On Friday we
sit in conference. The period of recess is devoted to opinion
writing and the study of appeals and certiorari petitions.

How much time does each Justice have at conference on Friday
of each argument week? Does conference discussion shed more
heat than light? What is the demeanor of the Justices? Let us
go from the austere courtroom—from the friezes depicting the
lawgivers, the Greek Ionic columns and the heavy draperies—to
the oak-paneled conference chamber and see what is going on
there. Over the mantel facing the large rectangular conference
table is a portrait of Chief Justice Marshall, the fourth Chief Justice by number, but the first in stature. Around this table are
nine chairs, each bearing the nameplate of a member of the
Court. At the east end sits the Chief Justice, and at the west,
Mr. Justice Black, the senior Associate Justice. On the sides, in

[*] From "The Supreme Court Conference," address before the Section on
Judicial Administration, American Bar Association, Dallas, Texas, August 27,
1956. Printed in 19 *Federal Rules Decisions* 303-310 (1956). Reprinted by
permission of Mr. Justice Clark.

order of seniority, sit the remaining Associate Justices. Book-
cases from floor to ceiling line the walls containing all the opinions
of the Federal courts. Here the Court meets in conference at
eleven A.M. on each Friday during or preceding an argument
week, and rarely does it rise before 5:30 P.M.

Only the Justices are present at conference. There are no
clerks, no stenographers, no secretaries, no pages. This long-estab-
lished practice is based on reason. The Court must carry on these
Friday conferences in absolute secrecy, otherwise its judgments
might become prematurely known and the whole process of
decision destroyed. We therefore guard its secrets closely. There
must be no leak. Scores of years ago the Court was convinced
that there was a leak. At that time two page boys waited on
the Justices within the conference room. After considerable investigation it was decided that the only possible leak was through
one of these lads. After all, no one else was present save the
Justices! So, since that day, no page—no person other than the
Justices themselves—has ever attended a conference. And this
despite the fact that thereafter a member of the bar advised the
Court that it was he who had provided the "leak." Basing his
conclusion of the outcome of a case purely on an educated guess,
he had sold a block of stock in a corporation involved in the
litigation on the very morning of the decision. His broker told
another of the sale leading to a run on the stock. But leak or
no leak, the Court ever since has stuck to the practice that only
Justices are present. . . .

Upon entering the conference room, each Justice shakes hands
with those present, another custom dating generations back. We
first take out our assignment sheets or lists for the day. As you
know, the only power of the Court is to decide lawsuits between
litigants with real interests at stake. The Court can proceed only
through the judicial process. This precludes the making of advisory opinions, even to the President. The Court is therefore a
passive instrument. Still the Court decided over 1800 questions
last term. There was an average of 71 cases on each list covering
the twenty-six conferences held during the term; the longest list
included 331 cases, the shortest 38. Our conferences last an
average of 6 hours, so this would allow on the average about five
minutes to each item on the list or half a minute to each Justice.
Perhaps this limited time brought Mr. Justice McReynolds to

the conclusion that an "overspeaking judge is no well-tuned cymbal." However, the Court is saved from being hopelessly bogged down by the elimination by consent of those cases that no Justice finds worthy of discussion.

What type of cases come up for discussion? First, appeals, then petitions for certiorari, next *informa pauperis* cases, and, more important than all, the cases argued previously in the courtroom. The Court always decides the latter cases the same week in which they were argued. I have made a hurried study of the legal problems presented last term. Aside from 13 original cases involving controversies between a third of our States, as well as the United States, we passed on 1831 cases. They posed legal questions running from adoption to zoning. As De Tocqueville predicted back in 1832, some of these were political questions turned, though sometimes clumsily, into judicial issues. There were questions concerning the Constitution, statutory construction, individual and States rights, Indians, labor, taxes, executive powers, contempt, seamen, railroad workers, subversives, bar applicants, as well as a host of other subjects.

The Chief Justice starts the conference by calling the first case on the list and then discussing it. He then yields to the senior Associate Justice and on down the line seniority-wise until each Justice who wishes to be heard has spoken. There is no time limitation. The order is never interrupted nor is the speaker. Another tale going the rounds of the Court has to do with a conference of many terms back while the late Justices Harlan and Holmes were on the Court. Harlan was presenting his view of a case with which Holmes evidently did not agree. In the midst of Harlan's argument, Holmes interrupted with the sharp remark, "That won't wash! That won't wash!" Justice Holmes often greeted Justice Harlan as "my strong hearted friend," but he had never chided him about his legal conclusions. Harlan too, was strong minded and never turned away from a fight. In this regard his opinions show that he wielded a wicked pair of horns and often got his adversary out on both of them. Holmes, on the other hand, was the rapier type that cut so quickly one did not know his head was off until he attempted to turn it. Fortunately, the Chief Justice at the time was Melville Fuller. He had already discussed the case and his position was similar to that of Harlan. When the diminutive but courageous, silver-haired, handlebar-mustached Chief Justice realized that all was not well between his brothers he quickly answered Holmes' "That won't wash," with a cheery "Well, I'm scrubbing away, anyhow." A tense situation passed over during the ensuing laughter.

After discussion of a case a vote is taken. We each have available a large docket book, evidently, from its appearance, handed down to us by the first of the Justices. It has a hinge on its flyleaf which is kept locked. There we keep a record of the votes. Ever since John Marshall's day the formal vote begins with the junior Justice and moves up through the ranks of seniority, the Chief Justice voting last. Hence the juniors are not influenced by the vote of their elders! While it takes five votes to decide a case, it takes only four to grant a writ of certiorari. In this manner, as Justice Van Devanter explained to the Congress back in 1925, the Court makes certain that any case deserving argument is afforded it. I might point out here that only sixteen percent of the petitions filed last term were granted. Less than two percent were state court cases. As the late revered Chief Justice Vinson said, "The Supreme Court has never been primarily concerned with the correction of errors in lower court decisions." The certiorari function, he continued, "is not simply to do justice between the parties. Everyone who comes here has had one trial and one appeal already." The purpose of the establishment of one Supreme National Tribunal was in the words of Chief Justice John Rutledge, "to secure the national rights and the uniformity of judgments." That is our mission. When you do not get four votes and certiorari is denied, it means your case did not come within the rule—not that the result is right.

As you see from this routine, each Justice who does not disqualify himself passes on every piece of business coming to the Court. In some matters Justices excuse themselves. This is always noted. Perhaps they were connected with the litigation before it reached the Court, had some interest in its result, or did not hear the argument because of unavoidable absence.

I wish to emphasize here that the Court does not function by means of committees or panels. Some lawyers think a small committee of Justices passes on their petitions for certiorari. This is not true. Each Justice passes on each petition, each item, no matter how drawn, in longhand, by typewriter, or on a press. Our

Constitution, as Brother Jackson has pointed out, "vests the judicial power in only 'one Supreme Court.'" This does not permit Supreme Court action by committees, panels, or sections. The method that the Justices use in meeting an enormous caseload such as last term varies. There is one uniform rule: Judging is not delegated. Each Justice studies each case in sufficient detail to resolve the question without leaving any doubt in his mind.

After the vote is recorded in argued cases there remains the task of writing the opinion for the Court. At the conclusion of the conference the cases are assigned for writing. The Chief Justice assigns those in which he has voted with the majority and the senior Justice voting with the majority the remainder. This has always been the rule. People often ask about the powers and duties of the Chief Justice. While it is not the purpose of this paper to cover that subject I might say that as to conference matters, aside from the duty of assigning opinions, the Chief Justice has no more authority than other members of the Court. The Chief Justice, of course, presides and initiates discussion, as a general rule, but has only one vote. However, the assignment of opinions is a most important duty. The manner of assignment varies as to courts. In New York State it goes by rotation. In one State, I am told, it goes by chance, while in others by subject matter.

When one starts to write an opinion for the Supreme Court of the United States he learns the full meaning of the statement of Rufus Choate that "one cannot drop the Greek alphabet to the ground and pick up the Iliad." It takes the most painstaking research and care. Mr. Justice Cardozo was not far wrong when he said, "A Judge must be a historian and prophet all in one." In the average case an opinion requires three weeks work in preparation. When the author concludes that he has an unanswerable document, it is printed in the print shop in the Supreme Court building and circulated to each of the Justices. Then the fur begins to fly. Returns come in, some favorable and many otherwise. In controversial cases, and all have some touches of controversy, the process often takes months. The cases are often discussed by the majority both before and after circulation. The final form of the opinion is agreed upon at the Friday conferences. Of course, any Justice may dissent or write his own views on a case. These are likewise circulated long before the opinion of the majority is announced. . . .

There will be, as always, some heat. Among judges, however, there is no contest, not even a "petty quarrel," but only a sincere and continuing effort to arrive at truth—at justice. As my Brother Frankfurter has so well put it: "What is essential in judging is . . . first and foremost, humility and an understanding of the range of the problems and [one's] own inadequacy in dealing with them: disinterestedness, allegiance to nothing except the search, amid tangled words, amid limited insights; loyalty and allegiance to nothing except the effort to find [that] path through precedent, through policy, through history, through [one's] own gifts of insight to the best judgment that a poor fallible creature can arrive at in that most difficult of all tasks, the adjudication between man and man, between man and state, through reason called law."

WILLIAM O. DOUGLAS

ASSOCIATE JUSTICE, 1939—

In Defense of Dissent[*]

All of us in recent years have heard and read many criticisms of the dissenting or concurring opinion. Separate opinions have often been deplored. Courts have been severely criticized for tolerating them. And that is why I rise to their defense.

About ten years ago when I took my seat on the bench, Chief Justice Hughes said this to me: "I think you will find after you have been on the bench for a while that in a great majority of the cases, perhaps in two-thirds of them, the judges will ultimately reach agreement and announce opinions that are unanimous. But in at least a third of the cases, agreement will not be possible. In those cases there will be dissents—no matter how carefully the judges are chosen—whether one president or several presidents selected them."

Chief Justice Hughes spoke from a long experience both at the Bar and in the Conference Room. What he said to me is important not only to judges and lawyers but to everyone in these days of uneasiness and confusion. It is indeed only when the meaning of his words is clear that the true nature of the judicial process is brought home to the community.

Holmes, perhaps better than anyone either before or after him, pointed out how illusory was the lawyer's search for certainty. Law is not what has been or is—law in the lawyer's sense is the prediction of things to come, the prediction of what decree will be written by designated judges on specified facts. In layman's language law is the prediction of what will happen to

* From "The Dissenting Opinion," address given before the Section on Judicial Administration, American Bar Association, Seattle, Washington, Sept. 9, 1948. Printed in Lawyer's Guild Review, Vol. 8, No. 6, November-December, 1948. Reprinted by permission of Mr. Justice Douglas and the publisher.

you if you do certain things. This was the lesson Holmes taught; and every lawyer on reflection knows that it is sound.

There are many reasons why this is so. No matter how clear and precise the code or other legal rule may be, the proof may be surrounded with doubt. And even though the proof is clear to advocate, the credibility of the witnesses may raise serious questions for judge or jury. Uncertainty is increased when new and difficult problems under ambiguous statutes arise. And when constitutional questions emerge, the case is, as we lawyers say, "at large." For the federal constitution, like most state constitutions, is not a code but a rule of action—a statement of philosophy and point of view, a summation of general principles, a delineation of the broad outlines of a regime which the Fathers designed for us.

These are the things that Holmes summed up when he described the lawyer's continuing and uncertain search for certainty. They indeed suggest why philosophers of the democratic faith will rejoice in the uncertainty of the law and find strength and glory in it.

Certainty and unanimity in the law are possible both under the fascist and communist systems. They are not only possible; they are indispensable. For complete subservience to the political regime is a *sine qua non* to judicial survival under either system. One cannot imagine the courts of Hitler engaged in a public debate over the principles of Der Fuehrer, with a minority of one of four deploring or denouncing the principles themselves. One cannot imagine a judge of a Communist court dissenting against the decree of the Kremlin.

Disagreement among judges is as true to the character of democracy as freedom of speech itself. The dissenting opinion is as genuinely American as Otis' denunciation of the general warrants, as Thomas Paine's, Thomas Jefferson's, or James Madison's briefs for civil liberties.

Democracy, like religion, is full of sects and schisms. Every political campaign demonstrates it. Every session of a legislature proves it. No man or group of men has a monopoly on truth, wisdom or virtue. An idea, once advanced for public acceptance, divides like an amoeba. The ifs and buts and howevers each claim a part; and what was once a whole is soon carved into many separate pieces, some of which are larger than even the original.

Those who have followed the legislative process can produce examples on end. That process is one of compromise—of qualifying absolutes, of creating exceptions to general rules. At times the process of compromise or conciliation involves wellnigh impossible adjustments. The clash of ideas may be so violent that a meeting of the minds seems out of the question. Where such cleavage is great and involves major issues, it may even tear a society apart. By the same token it can stop the legislative process or render it impotent, and thus deprive society of lawful and nonviolent means and methods of solving its problems. When the breach between the *pros* and *cons* is not too great, the legislative process functions. Even then, the compromise between competing ideas that merges in the final legislation may be more apparent than real. For the legislative solution is often to write two opposing ideas into a statute. Without that solution enactment of the measure might indeed be impossible.

And so the bill becomes the law and the law arrives before judges for interpretation. The battle that raged before the legislature is now transferred to the court. The passage of the legislation quieted the conflict only temporarily. It breaks out anew in the process of interpretation in the courts. A storm hits the court room, and the advocates take up the fight where the legislature left off. The same cleavage that appeared in legislative halls now shows up among the judges. Each side has eminent authority for its view since two conflicting ideas found their way into the legislation. It is therefore easy for judge or lawyer or editor to accuse the judges who take the opposing view of usurping the role of the legislature. A more honest, a more objective view would concede that interpretation has legislative as well as judicial characteristics. It cannot be otherwise where the legislature has left that choice of competing theories or ideas to the judges.

The legislative process breeds dissension among judges in other ways. An hiatus may be left in a law. The crucial matter may have been too explosive for the legislators to handle. For that or for other reasons they passed it over entirely or left it vague and undefined. The necessity to fill in the gap is then presented to the Court. And the judges are left at large in a field that the legislature lacked capacity to define. To a degree the same problem is presented to the judiciary when vague and general language is employed like the words "fair" or "just" or "equitable." The law is not a series of calculating machines where definitions and answers come tumbling out when the right levers are pushed. A judge's reaction to vague statutory language is bound to be like his reaction to the generalities of constitutional clauses. The language that he construes gathers meaning and overtones, significance and relevancy in terms of his own life and experience, his personal set of values, his training and education, and the genes of the blood stream of his ancestors. It would be as futile to argue that judges are not human as it would to prove that politics and legislatures can be divorced.

When we move to constitutional questions, uncertainty necessarily increases. A judge who is asked to construe or interpret the Constitution often rejects the gloss which his predecessors have put on it. For the gloss may in his view offend the spirit of the Constitution or do violence to it. That has been the experience of this generation and of all those that have preceded. It will likewise be the experience of those who follow. And so it should be. For it is the Constitution which we have sworn to defend, not some predecessor's interpretation of it. *Stare decisis* has small place in constitutional law. The Constitution was written for all times and all ages. It would lose its great character and become feeble, if it were allowed to become encrusted with narrow, legalistic notions that dominated the thinking of one generation.

So it is that the law will always teem with uncertainty. It has always been the case—and it always will remain that way under the democratic scheme of things. The truth is that the law is the highest form of compromise between competing interests; it is a substitute for force and violence—the only path to peace man has yet devised. It is the product of attempted reconciliation between the many diverse groups in a society. The reconciliation is not entirely a legislative function. The judiciary is also inescapably involved. When judges do not agree, it is a sign that they are dealing with problems on which society itself is divided. It is the democratic way to express dissident views. Judges are to be honored rather than criticized for following that tradition, for proclaiming their articles of faith so that all may read.

Chief Justice Hughes had this to say about the dissenting **opinion**:

There are some who think it desirable that dissents should not be disclosed as they detract from the forces of the judgment. Undoubtedly, they do. When unanimity can be obtained without sacrifice or coercion, it strongly commends the decision to public confidence. But unanimity which is merely formal, which is recorded at the expense of strong conflicting views, is not desirable in a court of last resort, whatever may be the effect upon public opinion at the time. This is so because what must ultimately sustain the court in public confidence is the character and independence of the judges. They are not there simply to decide cases, but to decide them as they think they should be decided, and while it may be regrettable that they cannot always agree, it is better that their independence should be maintained and recognized than that unanimity should be secured through its sacrifice. * * * A dissent in a court of last resort is an appeal to the brooding spirit of the law, to the intelligence of a future day, when a later decision may possibly correct the error into which the dissenting judge believes the court to have been betrayed.

That view was in the tradition of Thomas Jefferson who believed that the English practice of seriatim opinions was the desirable one. He thought each judge should write an opinion in every case so as to "throw himself in each case on God and his country; both will excuse him for error and value him for honesty."

The crises that face a democratic country under the stresses and strains of modern society are shared by judges. The judiciary is a coordinate branch of government, bearing great responsibilities. The judge that writes his own predilections into the law in disregard of constitutional principles or the legislative or executive edicts that he interprets is not worthy of the great traditions of the bench. The judge that quavers or retreats before an impending crisis of the day and finds haven in dialectics or weasel words or surrenders his own conviction for a passing expediency is likewise not born for the woolsack. We must expect of judges the fortitude and courage that we demand of all other servants who man our public posts. If they are true to their responsibilities and traditions, they will not hesitate to speak frankly and plainly on the great issues coming before them. They will prove their worth by showing their independence and fortitude. Their dissents or concurring opinions may salvage for tomorrow the principle that was sacrificed or forgotten today. Their discussion and propagation of the great principles of our Charter may keep the democratic ideal alive in days of regression, uncertainty and despair. Indeed what they do and say may in the manner of Holmes and Brandeis and Hughes have a more profound effect on the character of our government and the future of our country than the deeds of any other public servant. Moreover their cool detachment and courageous objectivity can set the fashion of a day and stamp an era with a distinctive character.

Archibald MacLeish recently wrote of this age:

> What's changed is freedom
> in this age—
> What great men dared to
> choose
> Small men now dare
> neither win
> Nor lose.

Judges, like other leaders of thought, must be free to choose—and, being free must have the daring to let their inner conscience cast their votes. They must be free to speak their minds—and the legal profession must help create an atmosphere of understanding and tolerance for their efforts.

In these critical days leaders in every walk of life must dare choose, publicly and with pride, our constitutional scheme of things in all its applications. They must dare choose it above all lesser things and reject the easy invitation of expediency or complacency. When the leaders make that choice, men of lesser stature and affairs will dare stake their all for freedom.

The Role of Oral Argument[*]

. . . I think that there is some tendency at the trial bar—I speak particularly from my knowledge of the trial bar of New York— to regard the oral argument as little more than a traditionally tolerated part of the appellate process. The view is widespread that when a court comes to the hard business of decision, it is the briefs, and not the oral argument, which count. . . . I think that view is a greatly mistaken one. It is quite different from the view at the English bar, for in England, appeals are still heard only on oral argument, without the submission of any briefs.

I do not mean to suggest that briefs do not play an important part in the appellate process. They do, of course, particularly where the litigation is a complicated one. But I think that the lawyer who depreciates the oral argument as an effective instrument of appellate advocacy, and stakes all on his brief, is making a great mistake. There are several reasons for this.

First of all, judges have different work habits. There are some judges who listen better than they read and who are more receptive to the spoken than the written word.

Secondly, the first impressions that a judge gets of a case are very tenacious. They frequently persist into the conference room. And those impressions are actually gained from the oral argument, if it is an effective job. While I was on the Court of Appeals, I kept a sort of informal scoreboard of the cases in

[*] From "What Part Does the Oral Argument Play in the Conduct of an Appeal?" address before the Judicial Conference of the Fourth Circuit, Asheville, North Carolina, June 24, 1955. Printed in 41 Cornell Law Quarterly 6 (1955). Reprinted by permission of Mr. Justice Harlan and the publisher.

which I sat so as to match up the initial reactions which I had to the cases after the close of the oral argument with the final reactions that I had when it came time to vote at the conferences on the decision of those cases. I was astonished to find during the year I sat on that Court how frequently—in fact, more times than not—the views which I had at the end of the day's session jibed with the final views that I formed after the more careful study of the briefs which, under our system in the Second Circuit, came in the period between the closing of the arguments and the voting at the conference.

Thirdly, the decisional process in many courts places a special burden on the oral argument. I am giving away no secrets, I am sure, when I say that in one of the Courts of Appeals where I was assigned to sit temporarily the voting on the cases took place each day following the close of the arguments. In the Supreme Court, our practice, as is well known, has been to hold our conferences at the end of each week of arguments. They have been on Saturdays up until now, but under a more enlightened schedule they will be on Fridays next term, because beginning October we are going to sit four days a week. Under either of those systems you can see the importance which the oral argument assumes.

Fourth, and to me this is one of the most important things, the job of courts is not merely one of an umpire in disputes between litigants. Their job is to search out the truth, both on the facts and the law, and that is ultimately the job of the lawyers, too. And in that joint effort, the oral argument gives an opportunity for interchange between court and counsel which the briefs do not give. For my part, there is no substitute, even within the time limits afforded by the busy calendars of modern appellate courts, for the Socratic method of procedure in getting at the real heart of an issue and in finding out where the truth lies.

Now, let me turn for a moment to some of the factors which seem to me to make for effective oral arguments. The art of advocacy—and it is an art—is a purely personal effort, and as such, any oral argument is an individualistic performance. Each lawyer must proceed according to his own lights, and if he tries to cast himself in the image of another, he is likely to become uneasy, artificial and unpersuasive. But after you make allowance for the special talents of individuals, their different methods of handling arguments, their different techniques, it seems to me that there are four characteristics which will be found in every effective oral argument, and they are these: *First*, what I would call selectivity; *Second*, what I would designate as simplicity; *Third*, candor; and *Fourth*, what I would term resiliency. Let me address myself briefly to each.

By "selectivity," I mean a lawyer's selection of the issues to be argued. There is rarely a case which lends itself to argument of all of the issues within the normal time limitations upon oral argument. On the other hand, there is hardly a case, however complicated, where, by some selection of the issues to be argued, one hour is not enough. I am not talking about the unusual type of case which we have from time to time in all courts where in the nature of things extra time is essential. But in most cases, I think, the skillful advocate would not want more time for oral argument than the ordinary rules of court permit. However, it often happens that lawyers who attempt to cover *all* of the issues in the case find themselves left with the uncomfortable feeling that they have failed to deal with any of the issues adequately. You will find that thoughtful selection of the issues to be argued orally is a basic technique of every good appellate advocate.

Most cases have one or only a few master issues. In planning his oral argument the wise lawyer will ferret out and limit himself to the issues which are really controlling, and will leave the less important or subordinate issues to the Court's own study of the briefs. Otherwise, one is apt to get tanglefoot, and the Court is left pretty much where it began.

The next thing I refer to is "simplicity." Simplicity of presentation and expression, you will find, is a characteristic of every effective oral argument. In the instances where that quality is lacking, it is usually attributable to one of two reasons—lack of preparation or poor selection of the issues to be argued. There are some issues that do not lend themselves to oral argument as well as they do to written presentation. The preparation of an oral argument is a good deal more than merely making a short form summary of the briefs. An oral argument which is no more than that really adds nothing to a lawyer's cause.

The process of preparation that the appellate advocate undergoes involves, *first*, the selection of the issues he will argue; *second*, a marshalling of the premises on which those issues depend;

third, planning the structure of his argument; and, *fourth*, deciding how he shall express his argument. It is sometimes forgotten by a lawyer who is full of his case, that the Court comes to it without the background that he has. And it is important to bear this in mind in carrying out the preparation for argument in each of its phases. Otherwise the force of some point which may seem so clear to the lawyer may be lost upon the Court.

The third thing which is of the essence of good advocacy is "candor." There is rarely a case, however strong, that does not have its weak points. And I do not know any way of meeting a weak point except to face up to it. It is extraordinary the number of instances one sees where through a question from the Court or the argument of one's adversary a vulnerable point is laid bare, and the wounded lawyer ducks, dodges and twists, instead of facing up to the point four square. Attempted evasion in an oral argument is a cardinal sin. No answer to an embarrassing point is better than an evasive one. With a Court, lack of candor in meeting a difficult issue of fact or of law goes far to destroying the effectiveness of a lawyer's argument, not merely as to the point of embarrassment, but often as to other points on which he should have the better of it. For if a lawyer loses the confidence of the court, he is apt to end up almost anywhere.

The fourth and final thing which I have suggested goes to the root of a good oral argument is "resiliency." For some reason that I have never been able to understand, many lawyers regard questioning by the court as a kind of subversive intrusion. And yet, when one comes to sit on the other side of the bar, he finds very quickly that the answer made to a vital question may be more persuasive in leading the Court to the right result than the most eloquent of oral arguments. I think that a lawyer, instead of shunning questions by the Court, should welcome them. If a court sits through an oral argument without asking any questions, it is often a pretty fair indication that the argument has been either dull or unconvincing.

I am mindful, of course, that the court's privilege of asking questions is sometimes abused, and that the price a lawyer has to pay is some interruption in the continuity of his argument, and perhaps some discomforture, and in extreme instances perhaps never getting through with what he had planned to say. And yet, I think that the price is well worth what the lawyer may have to pay in the loss of the smooth-flowering quality he would like his argument to have. A lawyer can make no greater mistake, I can assure you, in answering questions by the Court if he attempts to preserve the continuity of his argument by telling the judge who asks the question that he will come to it later. Usually, he never does. Or in saying, "Judge, I have dealt with that in my brief." Even if the lawyer does come back to the question later on, the force of his answer, if it is a good one, and often also of his argument in other aspects where he perhaps is in a stronger position, is usually lost—at least upon the judge who has asked the question.

No doubt some judges ask too many questions, and I hasten to say, again as one freshly from the trial bar, that I am one of those who believe that competent lawyers ought to be allowed to try their cases and argue their appeals in their own fashion. Where an over-enthusiastic judge exceeds the bounds of what the lawyer might consider fair interruption, the lawyer will have to handle that problem for himself. . . .

PART TWO

Court, Congress, and the States

"In the federal system there has been a healthy interplay between the courts and Congress. . . . There were at least 26 instances between 1945 and 1957 where Congress by later enactment modified or changed the rule of law announced by the Supreme Court. . . . The notion that the court that made the ruling which Congress changed went contrary to a common understanding of what the law meant is nonsense. The questions of which I speak are close ones, on which judges divide. . . . The truth is that the reach of a law may never be appreciated by the enacting body until it has been passed and put into practice . . . words are treacherous for the transmission of ideas. That is why constant legislative reappraisal of statutes as construed by the courts . . . is a healthy practice."

Mr. Justice Douglas

"Legislation has an aim; it seeks to obviate some mischief, to supply an inadequacy, to effect a change of policy, to formulate a plan of government. That aim, that policy, is not drawn, like nitrogen, out of the air; it is evinced in the language of the statute, as read in light of other external manifestations of purpose. That is what the judge must seek and effectuate, and he ought not to be led off the trail by tests that have overtones of subjective design. We do not delve into the mind of legislators or their draftsmen, or committee members."

Mr. Justice Frankfurter

"What is there to prevent Congress taking away, bit by bit, all the appellate jurisdiction of the Supreme Court of the United States, not doing it by direct attack but by [an] indirect attack? I see nothing. . . . That is the real loophole. What is the use of talking about limiting and fixing the number of justices so that the Court cannot be packed; what is the utility of saying justices must retire at a certain period so as not to have an old, tired, super-annuated Court; what is the good of providing that we shall make the Court less conscious of the political movements in the country by depriving the justices of the right to have any ambition for future office; if you leave the Court's appellate powers open to be dealt with and set aside by action of Congress in any given class of cases or in all cases which, traditionally, it has dealt with as the final appellate body under the Constitution?"

Former Justice Owen D. Roberts

"It is because the Supreme Court's review of state court decisions is limited to review of federal questions that a state judge coming to the Supreme Court learns that his state court experience has not always fully prepared him for his new work. . . . The state court judge who has dealt primarily with problems of property, contract, fault, crime, and zoning finds that he must sharpen his familiarity with the different bench marks that direct his judgments in the Supreme Court."

Mr. Justice Brennan

WILLIAM O. DOUGLAS

ASSOCIATE JUSTICE, 1939—

Judges and Legislators*

. . . Courts as an institution are too deeply fixed in our society to take a back seat. There is, I think, no sturdier element in the democratic system than an independent Judiciary. It reflects the need on the part of the lowliest for belief that justice is administered once the center of things is reached. Faith that in spite of delays, costs, and shenanigans justice is not for sale, justice is impartial, and justice can be had by the common man is an essential keystone in the arch of the system that sustains us. The winds of passion can play, mobs can march, riots can take place; but there is long-run stability once the judiciary is viewed as the great rock that is unmoved by the storms that break over it.

The storms that break by reason of constitutional decisions are sometimes so great as to lead to constitutional amendments or attempts at nullification. Yet the judicial check on executive and legislative action is not something that is becoming archaic. Quite the contrary. Article 56 of the new French Constitution establishes the Constitutional Council to pass on the constitutionality of laws. The Turkish Constitution provides for the Council of State to pass on the constitutionality of administrative actions of the government. India, Burma, and Pakistan provide for judicial review of the constitutionality of acts of the legislature. That power has been assumed by the Supreme Court of Canada and the Supreme Court of Australia. Despots dislike an independent judiciary. Once there is a written Constitution it is but a short step to the assertion of the power of judicial review—provided the

* From "Legal Institutions in America," speech at the Centennial of Columbia Law School, New York, N. Y., November 8, 1958. Printed in *Legal Institutions Today and Tomorrow*, New York, Columbia Univ., Monrad G. Paulsen, Ed. (1959), pp. 274ff. Reprinted by permission of Mr. Justice Douglas and the publisher.

society has democratic values. Then there is abiding force in the
statement of Marshall in *Marbury* v. *Madison*, 5 Cranch 137, 180,
". . . the framers of the Constitution contemplated that instrument as a rule for the government of courts, as well as of the
legislature. Why otherwise does it direct the judges to take an
oath to support it?"

Judicial review of the constitutionality of the actions of the
several States making up a federal system may not be essential to
the preservation of the federalism. But some federal referee is
necessary if States, which often have had parochial views, are not
to distort the constitutional scheme. What Madison wrote in
1831 needs repeating today:

> A supremacy of the Constitution & Laws of the Union, without
> a supremacy in the exposition & execution of them, would be as
> much a mockery as a scabbard put into the hand of a Soldier
> without a sword in it. I have never been able to see, that with-
> out such a view of the subject the Constitution itself could be
> the supreme law of the land; or that the *uniformity* of the Federal
> Authority throughout the parties to it could be preserved; or that
> without this *uniformity*, anarchy & disunion could be prevented.

The major work of courts—federal and state—deals not with
the Constitution but with the common law and with statutes.
Statutes are the mainstay of litigation in the federal courts. In
cases coming to the Supreme Court there are few which do not
involve a federal statute, obliquely if not directly. There was a
time when statutes were thought of as intruders; and the narrowest possible construction was given them. Sutherland in the
first edition of Statutes and Statutory Construction (1891) deplored "legislative interference" in law making. But those days
are gone. Statutes are now hospitably received. The days when
the judiciary was the paramount policy maker are over. The fact
that a transaction does not fall squarely within the statutory
prohibition is no longer a barrier to judicial action. The attitude
of the civil law toward statutes[1] is more and more followed by
other courts. An examination of current decisions in civil law
jurisdictions[2] indicates that their approach to statutory construction is not today basically different from the one federal judges
employ in construing Acts of Congress.

Courts seldom refrain from the difficult task of construction.

When they do so it is usually out of deference to an administrative agency whose expertise gives it the first say.[3]

We have no federal common law in the criminal field. Most of our civil litigation in the federal system also turns on statutory construction. Since *Erie R. Co.* v. *Tompkins*, 304 U. S. 64, our federal courts have ceased fashioning a federal common law in diversity cases. Now the architects of the governing substantive law in diversity litigation are the state courts. There still is some room in other types of cases for federal courts to fashion a federal common law governing some commercial transactions.[4] At times Congress has provided sanctions for enforcement of certain types of agreements, leaving to federal courts the fashioning of the federal substantive law to be applied.[5] That is in the great common law tradition. Of course a court deals with policy matters not only when it fashions substantive common law but when it determines rules of evidence, as for example, the propriety of a wife's testifying for or against her husband.[6] Federal courts are well-known policy-makers in other procedural matters touching the working of the federal court system.[7] The same is true when principles of liability are stated and restated in the admiralty field.[8] When the Court performs that function, it does not take a very great step from the role it fills in construing a rather vague statutory term such as restraint of trade.[9]

Of course, courts, when construing statutes, necessarily engage in a species of law-making. It is what Gray, *The Nature and Sources of the Law*, p. 173, called "legislating to fill up *casus omissi*." The legislature often does no more than provide a general standard. Much debate and nice speculations take place concerning the application of the law to a specific case. There is sometimes little light gained from canvassing legislative purpose. Congress may have spoken in harsh, mandatory terms, using "shall" instead of "may." Yet did it leave no room for the play of discretion?

Sometimes the law has evolved through a welter of enactments. To find through the maze the trail that marks the policy involves a profound search.

The main thrust of the legislative purpose may be clear; it is the case in the penumbra that causes difficulty.

There may be gaps that break the symmetry of the law; and judicial embroidery may be necessary to complete the motif.

The policy may be clear. Would Congress have gone as far as the courts are asked to go if it had thought of the precise case? It is no help to ask what Congress intended. Exploration of the minds of those who voted for it would be fruitless even if possible. It would moreover be beside the point, which is to ascertain the meaning of the words that were actually used. There are usually reliable records to show the purpose of the law. But these may be of little help. The full implications of what Congress did may never have been appreciated at the time. The application of·the law may have brought about the first clear realization of its perplexities. Or the compromise which ambiguous language effected in Congress may have merely delayed a settlement of the issue. Where Congress has not clearly chosen the path it wants to follow which should the courts prefer?

These are mainly minuscule problems of policy, as Justice Charles D. Breitel points out. The Court in construing a statute is not free to choose the policy it would prefer as it does when it fashions a common-law rule. Yet judges are human and every one of them is bound to see a problem through the windows of his own experience. One who once prosecuted under laws enforcing the Commerce Clause is apt to read the words "interstate commerce" more expansively than one who spent his years at the Bar defending local interests. But that is the beginning not the end of the problem. A judge worthy of the tradition does not draw from the well of his prejudices in construing statutory words. It would be as much a subversion of the judicial function for him to read his predilections into a statute as it would to use Due Process to put his own social philosophy into the Constitution. The problem is to stick with the legislative scheme and determine which construction is most consonant with it. Even when this is done, judges sharply divide and will continue to do so. For these marginal questions in the law are so inherently provocative as to breed differences of opinion.

What may be the clear meaning of words to some create ambiguities for others. The truth is that, while we start with the words of the Act, that is the beginning, not the end of the search. For words are inexact tools to say the least.

Most American judges look beyond the words to ascertain what occasioned the law and to learn what evil the enactment was designed to eradicate. There was a time when only the word of the spokesmen for the measure or the Committee report was considered.[10] Those are still the most authoritative pronouncements of legislative purpose. But the recent tendency in the federal system has been to ransack the entire legislative history for what light can be thrown on the problem of interpretation.[11] More and more does the search for the meaning of words take one through the morass of legislative history, looking for help from any competent source. This is a delicate task requiring much evaluation. Unless carefully done it can lead to treacherous results. For some legislative history is artfully made to serve a selfish purpose. Judges, however, are aware of the problem.[12]

Some questions of statutory construction have constitutional overtones. I refer not only to strained constructions made to avoid constitutional adjudications. I include also those cases that pose the question whether the purpose of Congress in enacting the law was to displace state law. If so, the Supremacy Clause comes into play. That search often involves many imponderables. It is frequently an issue on which judges sharply divide.[13] Double regulation—both by state and federal laws—may be logically permissible but practically unsound. Dual regulation may be inherently so disruptive of the policy of the federal law that the purpose of Congress to foreclose state action may be implied.

In all cases of statutory construction—those that involve the Supremacy Clause as well as the others—the legislature has the final word. If the congressional will is defied, the error can be corrected by an amendment of the law.

In the federal system there has been a healthy interplay between the courts and the Congress. One conspicuous example concerns the income tax where Committees of the Congress prepare a new law every two years. Moreover the Joint Committee on Internal Revenue Taxation and its highly efficient technical staff keep the judicial interpretations of the Internal Revenue Code under continuous scrutiny. Those decisions accordingly come up almost routinely for evaluation. The number that are prospectively changed or modified would add up to a healthy total over the period of a decade. A recent study indicates that apart from internal revenue cases, there were at least 26 instances between 1945 and 1957 where Congress by later enactment modified or changed the rule of law announced by the Supreme Court. 71 Harv. L. Rev. 1324. At times Congress may be expressing disagreement with a policy that an earlier Congress approved. Congress may be taking into account policy considerations which were inappropriate for the judiciary to consider. Congress with the benefit of hindsight may desire to limit the full thrust of an earlier law. The notion that the court that made the ruling which Congress changed went contrary to a common understanding of what the law meant is nonsense. The questions of which I speak are close ones, on which judges divide. To be sure, some judicial construction has been so hostile to the statutory scheme as to change its character and greatly weaken it. Such was the history of the Federal Employer's Liability Act, all as related in H. R. Rep. No. 1222, 76th Cong., 1st Sess. Congress then restored the law as it was before the judges changed it. That history, which sometimes seems to repeat itself [14] is a lively influence in the close judicial scrutiny now given to FELA cases. But that illustration is a unique one. Judges, like other people, have a difficult time in ridding themselves of habits of thought. But I do not know of a judiciary that is perverse. The truth is that the reach of a law may never be appreciated by the enacting body until it has been passed and put into practice. Congress is not omniscient; no matter how careful the draftsmen, all contingencies cannot possibly be foreseen; words are treacherous for the transmission of ideas. That is why constant legislative reappraisal of statutes as construed by the courts—such as we have in the case of the Internal Revenue Code—is a healthy practice.[15]

We are apt to think of judges when we think of human rights. But the courts have not always hewn to the line. During recent years there has been a sharp decline in respect for civil rights as the search for the subversive gained momentum. That decline was manifest in court decisions. It was conspicuous also in the administrative agency field. The whole loyalty program for government employees was indeed based on complicated and treacherous procedures before various agencies. Legislatures with their investigating committees also beat the drums of intolerance, also took short-cuts that were not in harmony with our principles.

Yet in the long view, legislatures and other conventions of the people deserve much credit for the fostering of civil rights. In the main the courts' record as guardian of those rights has been good. The genius of the judiciary in fashioning the writ of *habeas corpus* as a check on arbitrary power is one example. So are the decisions protecting civilians against military trials, the numerous rulings which outlaw devices to disenfranchise Negroes or to perpetuate racial discrimination, the banning of confessions obtained by coercion, the requirement of counsel, and so on. The list is long and striking. But when one looks down the long vista of Anglo-American history he learns that as many, if not more, victories for freedom were won in legislatures and conventions as in the courts. When it comes to human rights, we owe more than we commonly acknowledge to legislative law, as Prof. Frank C. Newman has reminded us. Legislators have also been good guardians of liberty. They have curbed judges who at times have proved to be tyrants as the history of the law of contempt particularly shows. Their creative genius has designed many bills of rights for the common man.

Some modern democracies place the legislature in a dominant position. Such is the British system. But that system is not ours. The separation of powers is basic to our institutions. Thus the great office of the President, like the Judiciary, must remain vigorously independent if it is to fulfill its historic missions.

There are periods in our history when we witness legislative encroachments. Woodrow Wilson in *Congressional Government* noted that trend. A cabal of congressmen sometimes bring a great executive department to heel, virtually dictating its policy. The power to investigate, that knows no restraint can be powerful indeed. Coupled with the power over the purse strings it gives great leverage. Legislative power has sometimes been asserted to control what in terms seemed to be rights that had been placed by the Constitution beyond the reach of regulations. Two recent examples are First Amendment rights and the rights of citizenship bestowed by the Fourteenth Amendment. In each instance Congress reached out to regulate those rights. These assertions of legislative power have in part been sustained by the Judiciary.[16] But that kind of legislative invasion is not our main derangement. They illustrate the ebb and flow of power. They are not major changes in the concept of separation of powers. The stature of Congress like that of the Presidency will depend on the character of the incumbents. It will also depend on the extent to which real power is transferred through numerous channels to the various cliques, groups, and blocs that make up "We The People."

Officials who do not echo public opinion may not be re-elected.

Officials who do no more than echo it may be paralyzed into inaction or propelled down false trails. On the great issues of foreign policy, international trade, war or peace, public opinion is often years behind. It is the least versatile on those complex, impersonal issues. It may be so drugged on the emotionalism of some issues, such as foreign policy, as to be incapable of intelligent decision on problems that spell the difference between survival and destruction. A serious malady affects democratic societies when their leaders are led or propelled by mass opinion which is not informed or conditioned to existing facts. Equally fatal is the plight of those listening for the voice of the people and hearing such a babel that they only drift with the tides. This might be called the major derangement of the democracies in this twentieth century.[17] The fact that we may not even be aware that this phenomenon operates dangerously in our midst is evidence of the seriousness of the malady.

These are matters that go to the very vitals of our way of life. The remedy lies in a public attitude or philosophy. Are we to be a mature integrated people approaching problems in a civilized way? If so, then the press must be more than free in the constitutional sense. The press must use its freedom to be versatile and at home in the world of ideas and not serve merely as instruments for propagating the prejudices of its owners. The family, the schools, and churches must prepare oncoming generations for a world of great diversity where one can live with intellectual excitement. We must as a people become more civilized in our attitudes, subduing the baser man for the common good and subjecting ourselves to great discipline and our quarrels, big and small, to a rule of law.

We need to develop a climate of opinion that produces men capable of speaking for "the inner consciousness" of the people, as Lord Denning put it. Some nations have known rulers who adapted itself to changing conditions and provided progressive leadership. We must find our aristocracy in men of learning and character who live and think above the requirements of precinct politics. This means a reversal of the leveling process we have experienced as we were more and more overwhelmed by conformity.

REFERENCES

[1] See Pound, "The Theory of Judicial Decision," 36 *Harvard Law Review* 647.
[2] See *Galloway v. Wyatt Metal & Boiler Works*, 189 La. 837; *State ex rel. Thompson v. Dept. of City Civil Service*, 214 La. 683.
[3] *Armour & Co. v. Alton R. Co.*, 312 U. S. 195.
[4] *Clearfield Trust Co. v. United States*, 318 U. S. 363.
[5] *Textile Workers Union v. Lincoln Mills*, 353 U. S. 448.
[6] *Funk v. United States*, 290 U. S. 371.
[7] *McNabb v. United States*, 318 U. S. 332.
[8] *Pope & Talbot, Inc., v. Hawn*, 346 U. S. 406, 409.
[9] *Standard Oil Co. of New Jersey v. United States*, 221 U. S. 1.
[10] *United States v. St. Paul, M. & M. R. Co.*, 247 U. S. 310, 318.
[11] *Schwegmann Bros. v. Calvert Corp.*, 341 U. S. 384; *Nashville Milk Co. v. Carnation Co.*, 355 U. S. 373; *United States v. C. I. O.*, 335 U. S. 106, 113.
[12] *United States v. American Trucking Assns.*, 310 U. S. 534, 544.
[13] *Hines v. Davidowitz*, 312 U. S. 52; *Rice v. Santa Fe Elevator Corp.*, 331 U. S. 218; *Pennsylvania v. Nelson*, 350 U. S. 497.
[14] *Tiller v. Atlantic Coast Line R. Co.*, 318 U. S. 54.
[15] There are recent examples of speedy exercise of this power by Congress when the desire to change an announced rule was strong. *Estate of Spiegel v. Commissioner*, 335 U. S. 701, was changed 9 months later by the Technical Changes Act of 1949 (63 Stat. 394); *Anderson v. Mt. Clemens Pottery Co.*, 328 U. S. 680, was changed 11 months later by the Portal-to-Portal Act of 1947 (61 Stat. 84).
[16] *Dennis v. United States*, 341 U. S. 494; *Perez v. Brownell*, 356 U. S. 44.
[17] See Lippman, *The Public Philosophy*.

FELIX FRANKFURTER

ASSOCIATE JUSTICE, 1939—

Reflections on Reading Statutes*

A single volume of 320 octavo pages contains all the laws passed by Congress during its first five years, when measures were devised for getting the new government under way; 26 acts were passed in the 1789 session, 66 in 1790, 94 in 1791, 38 in 1792, 63 in 1793. For the single session of the 70th Congress, to take a pre-depression period, there are 993 enactments in a monstrous volume of 1014 pages—quarto not octavo—with a comparable range of subject matter. . . . Inevitably the work of the Supreme Court reflects the great shift in the center of gravity of law-making. Broadly speaking, the number of cases disposed of by opinions has not changed from term to term. But even as late as 1875 more than 40 per cent of the controversies before the Court were common-law litigation, fifty years later only 5 per cent, while today cases not resting on statutes are reduced almost to zero. It is therefore accurate to say that courts have ceased to be the primary makers of law in the sense in which they "legislated" the common law. It is certainly true of the Supreme Court, that almost every case has a statute at its heart or close to it.

This does not mean that every case before the Court involves questions of statutory construction. If only literary perversity or jaundiced partisanship can sponsor a particular rendering of a statute there is no problem. When we talk of statutory construction we have in mind cases in which there is a fair contest between

* From the Benjamin N. Cardozo Lecture before the Association of the Bar of the City of New York, March, 18, 1947, printed in The Record of the Association, Vol. 2 (June 1947), pp. 213-237. Reprinted by permission of Mr. Justice Frankfurter and the publisher.

two readings, neither of which comes without respectable title deeds. A problem in statutory construction can seriously bother courts only when there is a contest between probabilities of meaning.

DIFFICULTIES OF CONSTRUCTION

Though it has its own preoccupations and its own mysteries and above all its own jargon, judicial construction ought not to be torn from its wider, non-legal context. Anything that is written may present a problem of meaning, and that is the essence of the business of judges in construing legislation. The problem derives from the very nature of words. They are symbols of meaning. But unlike mathematical symbols, the phrasing of a document, especially a complicated enactment, seldom attains more than approximate precision. If individual words are inexact symbols, with shifting variables, their configuration can hardly achieve invariant meaning or assured definiteness. Apart from the ambiguity inherent in its symbols, a statute suffers from ċ··bieties. It is not an equation or a formula representing a clearly ıarked process, nor is it an expression of individual thought to which is imparted the definiteness a single authorship can give. A statute is an instrument of government partaking of its practical purposes but also of its infirmities and limitations, of its awkward and groping efforts. . . .

The difficulties are inherent not only in the nature of words, of composition, and of legislation generally. They are often intensified by the subject matter of an enactment. The imagination which can draw an income tax statute to cover the myriad transactions of a society like ours, capable of producing the necessary revenue without producing a flood of litigation, has not yet revealed itself. . . . Moreover, government sometimes solves problems by shelving them temporarily. The legislative process reflects that attitude. Statutes as well as constitutional provisions at times embody purposeful ambiguity or are expressed with a generality for future unfolding. "The prohibition contained in the Fifth Amendment refers to infamous crimes—a term obviously inviting interpretation in harmony with conditions and opinions prevailing from time to time."[1] And Mr. Justice Cardozo once remarked, "a great principle of constitutional law is not susceptible of comprehensive statement in an adjective."[2]

The intrinsic difficulties of language and the emergence after enactment of situations not anticipated by the most gifted legislative imagination, reveal doubts and ambiguities in statutes that
compel judicial construction. The process of construction, therefore, is not an exercise in logic or dialectic. The aids of formal
reasoning are not irrelevant; they may simply be inadequate. The
purpose of construction being the ascertainment of meaning,
every consideration brought to bear for the solution of that problem must be devoted to that end alone. To speak of it as a
practical problem is not to indulge a fashion in words. It must
be that, not something else. Not, for instance, an opportunity for
a judge to use words as "empty vessels into which he can pour
anything he will"—his caprices, fixed notions, even statesmanlike
beliefs in a particular policy. Nor, on the other hand, is the process a ritual to be observed by unimaginative adherence to well-
worn professional phrases. To be sure, it is inescapably a problem
in the keeping of the legal profession and subject to all the limitations of our adversary system of adjudication. When the judge,
selected by society to give meaning to what the legislature has
done, examines the statute, he does so not in a laboratory or in
a classroom. Damage has been done or exactions made, interests
are divided, passions have been aroused, sides have been taken.
But the judge, if he is worth his salt, must be above the battle.
We must assume in him not only personal impartiality but intellectual disinterestedness. In matters of statutory construction
also it makes a great deal of difference whether you start with
an answer or with a problem.

THE JUDGE'S TASK

Everyone has his own way of phrasing the task confronting
judges when the meaning of a statute is in controversy. Judge
Learned Hand speaks of the art of interpretation as "the prolifera-
tion of purpose." Who am I not to be satisfied with Learned
Hand's felicities? And yet that phrase might mislead judges intellectually less disciplined than Judge Hand. It might justify interpretations by judicial libertines, not merely judicial libertarians.
My own rephrasing of what we are driving at is probably no more
helpful, and is much longer, than Judge Hand's epigram. I
should say that the troublesome phase of construction is the determination of the extent to which extraneous documentation and

external circumstances may be allowed to infiltrate the text on the theory that they were part of it, written in ink discernible to the judicial eye.

Chief Justice White was happily endowed with the gift of finding the answer to problems by merely stating them. Often have I envied him this faculty but never more than in recent years. No matter how one states the problem of statutory construction, for me, at least, it does not carry its own answer. Though my business throughout most of my professional life has been with statutes, I come to you empty-handed. I bring no answers. I suspect the answers to the problems of an art are in its exercise. Not that one does not inherit, if one is capable of receiving it, the wisdom of the wise. But I confess unashamedly that I do not get much nourishment from books on statutory construction, and I say this after freshly re-examining them all, scores of them.

When one wants to understand, or at least get the feeling of, great painting, one does not go to books on the art of painting. One goes to the great masters. . . .

And so I have examined the opinions of Holmes, Brandeis and Cardozo and sought to derive from their treatment of legislation what conclusions I could fairly draw, freed as much as I could be from impressions I had formed in the course of the years.

Holmes came to the Supreme Court before the great flood of recent legislation, while the other two, especially Cardozo, appeared at its full tide. The shift in the nature of the Court's business led to changes in its jurisdiction, resulting in a concentration of cases involving the legislative process. Proportionately to their length of service and the number of opinions, Brandeis and Cardozo had many more statutes to construe. And the statutes presented for their interpretation became increasingly complex, bringing in their train a quantitatively new role for administrative regulations. Nevertheless, the earliest opinions of Holmes on statutory construction, insofar as he reveals himself, cannot be distinguished from Cardozo's last opinion, though the latter's process is more explicit.

A judge of marked individuality stamps his individuality on what he writes, no matter what the subject. What is however striking about the opinions of the three Justices in this field is the essential similarity of their attitude and of their appraisal of the relevant. Their opinions do not disclose a private attitude for or against extension of governmental authority by legislation, or towards the policy of particular legislation, which consciously or imperceptibly affected their judicial function in construing laws. It would thus be a shallow judgment that found in Mr. Justice Holmes' dissent in the *Northern Securities* case (193 U. S. 197, 400) an expression of his disapproval of the policy behind the Sherman Law. His habit of mind—to be as accurate as one can be—had a natural tendency to confine what seemed to him familiar language in a statute to its familiar scope. But the proof of the pudding is that his private feelings did not lead him to invoke the rule of indefiniteness to invalidate legislation of which he strongly disapproved (Compare *Nash* v. *United States,* 229 U. S. 373, and *International Harvester Co.* v. *Kentucky,* 234 U. S. 216), or to confine language in a constitution within the restrictions which he gave to the same language in a statute. (Compare *Towne* v. *Eisner,* 245 U. S. 418, and *Eisner* v. *Macomber,* 252 U. S. 189.)

The reservations I have just made indicate that such differences as emerge in the opinions of the three Justices on statutory construction, are differences that characterize all of their opinions, whether they are concerned with interpretation or constitutionality, with admiralty or patent law. They are differences of style. In the case of each, the style is the man.

If it be suggested that Mr. Justice Holmes is often swift, if not cavalier, in his treatment of statutes, there are those who level the same criticism against his opinions generally. It is merited in the sense that he wrote, as he said, for those learned in the art. I need hardly add that for him "learned" was not a formal term comprehending the whole legal fraternity. When dealing with problems of statutory construction also he illumined whole areas of doubt and darkness with insights enduringly expressed, however briefly. To say "We agree to all the generalities about not supplying criminal laws with what they omit, but there is no canon against using commonsense in construing laws as saying what they obviously mean," *Roschen* v. *Ward,* 279 U. S. 337, 339, is worth more than most of the dreary writing on how to construe penal legislation. Again when he said that "the meaning of a sentence is to be felt rather than to be proved," *United States* v. *Johnson,* 221 U. S. 488, 496, he expressed the wholesome truth that the final rendering of the meaning of a statute is an act of judgment. He would shudder at the thought that by such a statement he was giving comfort to the school of visceral jurisprudence. Judgment is not drawn out of the void but is based on the correlation of imponderables all of which need not, because they cannot, be made explicit. He was expressing the humility of the intellectual that he was, whose standards of exactitude distrusted pretensions of certainty, believing that legal controversies that are not frivolous almost always involve matters of degree, and often degree of the nicest sort. Statutory construction implied the exercise of choice, but precluded the notion of capricious choice as much as choice based on private notions of policy. One gets the impression that in interpreting statutes Mr. Justice Holmes reached meaning easily, as was true of most of his results, with emphasis on the language in the totality of the enactment and the felt reasonableness of the chosen construction. He had a lively awareness that a statute was expressive of purpose and policy, but in his reading of it he tended to hug the shores of the statute itself, without much re-enforcement from without.

Mr. Justice Brandeis, on the other hand, in dealing with these problems as with others, would elucidate the judgment he was exercising by proof or detailed argument. In such instances, especially when in dissent, his opinions would draw on the whole arsenal of aids to construction. More often than either Holmes or Cardozo, Brandeis would invoke the additional weight of some "rule" of construction. But he never lost sight of the limited scope and function of such "rules." Occasionally, however, perhaps because of the nature of a particular statute, the minor importance of its incidence, the pressure of judicial business or even the temperament of his law clerk, whom he always treated as a co-worker, Brandeis disposed of a statute even more dogmatically, with less explicit elucidation, than did Holmes.

For Cardozo, statutory construction was an acquired taste. He preferred common law subtleties, having great skill in bending them to modern uses. But he came to realize that problems of statutory construction had their own exciting subtleties and gave ample employment to philosophic and literary talents. Cardozo's elucidation of how meaning is drawn out of a statute gives proof of the wisdom and balance which, combined with his learning, made him a great judge. While the austere style of Brandeis seldom mitigated the dry aspect of so many problems of statutory construction, Cardozo managed to endow even these with the warmth and softness of his writing. The differences in the tone and color of their style as well as in the moral intensity of Brandeis and Cardozo made itself felt when they wrote full-dress opinions on problems of statutory construction. Brandeis almost compels by demonstration; Cardozo woos by persuasion.

SCOPE OF THE JUDICIAL FUNCTION

From the hundreds of cases in which our three Justices construed statutes one thing clearly emerges. The area of free judicial movement is considerable. These three remembered that laws are not abstract propositions. They are expressions of policy arising out of specific situations and addressed to the attainment of particular ends. The difficulty is that the legislative ideas which laws embody are both explicit and immanent. And so the bottom problem is: What is below the surface of the words and yet fairly a part of them? Words in statutes are not unlike words in a foreign language in that they too have "associations, echoes, and overtones." [3] Judges must retain the associations, hear the echoes, and capture the overtones. In one of his very last opinions, dealing with legislation taxing the husband on the basis of the combined income of husband and wife, Holmes wrote: "The statutes are the outcome of a thousand years of history. . . . They form a system with echoes of different moments, none of which is entitled to prevail over the other." [4]

What exactions such a duty of construction places upon judges, and with what freedom it entrusts them! John Chipman Gray was fond of quoting from a sermon by Bishop Hoadley that "Whoever hath an *absolute authority* to *interpret* any written or spoken laws, it is he who is truly the law-giver to all intents and purposes, and not the person who first wrote or spoke them." Gray, Nature and Sources of the Law (2nd ed. 1921) 102, 125, 172. By admitting that there is some substance to the good Bishop's statement, one does not subscribe to the notion that they are law-givers in any but a very qualified sense.

Even within their area of choice the courts are not at large. They are confined by the nature and scope of the judicial function in its particular exercise in the field of interpretation. They are under the constraints imposed by the judicial function in our democratic society. As a matter of verbal recognition certainly, no one will gainsay that the function in construing a statute is to ascertain the meaning of words used by the legislature. To go beyond it is to usurp a power which our democracy has lodged in its elected legislature. The great judges have constantly admonished their brethren of the need for discipline in observing the limitations. A judge must not rewrite a statute, neither to enlarge nor to contract it. Whatever temptations the statesmanship of policymaking might wisely suggest, construction must eschew interpolation and evisceration. He must not read in by way of creation. He must not read out except to avoid patent nonsense or internal contradiction. "If there is no meaning in it," said Alice's King, "that saves a world of trouble, you know, as we needn't try to find any." Legislative words presumably have meaning and so we must try to find it.

This duty of restraint, this humility of function as merely the translator of another's command, is a constant theme of our Justices. It is on the lips of all judges, but seldom, I venture to believe, has the restraint which it expresses, or the duty which it enjoins, been observed with so consistent a realization that its observance depends on self-conscious discipline. Cardozo put it this way: "We do not pause to consider whether a statute differently conceived and framed would yield results more consonant with fairness and reason. We take this statute as we find it." [5] It was expressed more fully by Mr. Justice Brandeis when the temptation to give what might be called a more liberal interpretation could not have been wanting: "The particularization and detail with which the scope of each provision, the amount of the tax thereby imposed, and the incidence of the tax, were specified, preclude an extension of any provision by implication to any other subject. . . . What the Government asks is not a construction of a statute, but, in effect, an enlargement of it by the court, so that what was omitted, presumably by inadvertence, may be included within its scope." [6] An omission, at the time of enactment, whether careless or calculated, cannot be judicially supplied however much later wisdom may recommend the inclusion.

The vital difference between initiating policy, often involving a decided break with the past, and merely carrying out a formulated policy, indicates the relatively narrow limits within which choice is fairly open to courts and the extent to which interpreting law is inescapably making law. To say that, because of this restricted field of interpretive declaration, courts make law just as do legislatures is to deny essential features in the history of our democracy. It denies that legislation and adjudication have had different lines of growth, serve vitally different purposes, function under different conditions, and bear different responsibilities. The judicial process of dealing with words is not at all Alice in Wonderland's way of dealing with them. Even in matters legal some words and phrases, though very few, approach mathematical symbols and mean substantially the same to all who have occasion to use them. Other law terms like "police power" are not symbols at all but labels for the results of the whole process of adjudication. In between lies a gamut of words with different denotations as well as connotations. There are varying shades of compulsion for judges behind different words, differences that are due to the words themselves, their setting in a text, their setting in history. In short, judges are not unfettered glossators. They are under a special duty not to overemphasize the episodic aspects of life and not to undervalue its organic processes—its continuities and relationships. For judges at least it is important to remember that continuity with the past is not only a necessity but even a duty.

There are not wanting those who deem naive the notion that judges are expected to refrain from legislating in construing statutes. They may point to cases where even our three Justices apparently supplied an omission or engrafted a limitation. Such an accusation cannot be rebutted or judged in the abstract. In some ways, as Holmes once remarked, every statute is unique. Whether a judge does violence to language in its total context is not always free from doubt. Statutes come out of the past and aim at the future. They may carry implicit residues or mere hints of purpose. Perhaps the most delicate aspect of statutory construction is not to find more residues than are implicit nor purposes beyond the bound of hints. Even for a judge most sensitive to the traditional limitation of his function, this is a matter for judgment not always easy of answer. But a line does exist between omission and what Holmes called "misprision or abbreviation that does not conceal the purpose." [7] Judges may differ as to the point at which the line should be drawn, but the only sure safeguard against crossing the line between adjudication and legislation is an alert recognition of the necessity not to cross it and instinctive, as well as trained, reluctance to do so.

In the realms where judges directly formulate law because the chosen lawmakers have not acted, judges have the duty of adaptation and adjustment of old principles to new conditions. But where policy is expressed by the primary law-making agency in a democracy, that is by the legislature, judges must respect such expressions by adding to or subtracting from the explicit terms which the lawmakers used no more than is called for by the shorthand nature of language. Admonitions, like that of Justice Brandeis in the *Iselin* case, that courts should leave even desirable enlargement to Congress will not by itself furnish the meaning appropriate for the next statute under scrutiny. But as is true of other important principles, the intensity with which it is believed may be decisive of the outcome.

THE PROCESS OF CONSTRUCTION

Let me descend to some particulars.

The text.—Though we may not end with the words in construing a disputed statute, one certainly begins there. You have a right to think that a hoary platitude, but it is a platitude too often not observed at the bar. In any event, it may not take you to the end of the road. The Court no doubt must listen to the voice of Congress. But often Congress cannot be heard clearly because its speech is muffled. Even when it has spoken, it is as true of Congress as of others that what is said is what the listener hears. Like others, judges too listen with what psychologists used to call the apperception mass, which I take it means in plain English that one listens with what is already in one's head. One more caution is relevant when one is admonished to listen attentively to what a statute says. One must also listen attentively to what it does not say.

We must, no doubt, accord the words the sense in which Congress used them. That is only another way of stating the central problem of decoding the symbols. It will help to determine for whom they were meant. Statutes are not archaeological documents to be studied in a library. They are written to guide the actions of men. As Mr. Justice Holmes remarked upon some Indian legislation "The word was addressed to the Indian mind," *Fleming v. McCurtain*, 215 U. S. 56, 60. If a statute is written for ordinary folk, it would be arbitrary not to assume that Congress intended its words to be read with the minds of ordinary men. If they are addressed to specialists, they must be read by judges with the minds of the specialists.

And so we assume that Congress uses common words in their popular meaning, as used in the common speech of men. The cases speak of the "meaning of common understanding," "the normal and spontaneous meaning of language," "the common and appropriate use," "the natural straightforward and literal sense," and similar variants. In *McBoyle* v. *United States*, 283 U. S. 25, 26, Mr. Justice Holmes had to decide whether an aeroplane is a "motor vehicle" within the meaning of the Motor Vehicle Theft Act. He thus disposed of it: "No doubt etymologically it is possible to use the word to signify a conveyance working on land, water or air, and sometimes legislation extends the use in that direction. . . . But in everyday speech 'vehicles' calls up a picture of a thing moving on land."

Sometimes Congress supplies its own dictionary. It did so in 1871, in a statute defining a limited number of words for use as to all future enactments. It may do so, as in recent legislation, by a section within a statute containing definitions for that statute. Or, there may be indications from the statute that words in it are employed in a distinctive sense. "If Congress has been accustomed to use a certain phrase with a more limited meaning than might be attributed to it by common practice, it would be arbitrary to refuse to consider that fact when we come to interpret a statute. But, as we have said, the usage of Congress simply shows that it has spoken with careful precision, that its words mark the exact spot at which it stops." [8] Or, words may acquire scope and function from the history of events which they summarize or from the purpose which they serve.

However colloquial and uncertain the words had been in the beginning, they had won for themselves finally an acceptance and a definiteness that made them fit to play a part in the legislative process. They came into the statute . . . freighted with the meaning imparted to them by the mischief to be remedied and by contemporaneous discussion. . . . In such conditions history is a teacher that is not to be ignored.

Words of art bring their art with them. They bear the meaning of their habitat whether it be a phrase of technical significance in the scientific or business world, or whether it be loaded with the recondite connotations of feudalism. Holmes made short shrift of a contention by remarking that statutes used "familiar legal expressions in their familiar legal sense." [10] The peculiar idiom of business or of administrative practise often modifies the meaning that ordinary speech assigns to language. And if a word is obviously transplanted from another legal source, whether the common law or other legislation, it brings the old soil with it.

The context.—Legislation is a form of literary composition. But construction is not an abstract process equally valid for every composition, not even for every composition whose meaning must be judicially ascertained. The nature of the composition demands awareness of certain pre-suppositions. For instance, the words in a constitution may carry different meanings from the same words in a statute precisely because "it is a constitution we are expounding." The reach of this consideration was indicated by Mr. Justice Holmes in language that remains fresh no matter how often repeated:

. . . when we are dealing with words that also are a constituent act, like the Constitution of the United States, we must realize that they have called into life a being the development of which could not have been foreseen completely by the most gifted of its begetters. It was enough for them to realize or to hope that they had created an organism; it has taken a century and has cost their successors much sweat and blood to prove that they created a nation. The case before us must be considered in the light of our whole experience and not merely in that of what was said a hundred years ago." [11]

And so, the significance of an enactment, its antecedents as well as its later history, its relation to other enactments, all may be relevant to the construction of words for one purpose and in one setting but not for another. Some words are confined to their history; some are starting points for history. Words are intellectual and moral currency. They come from the legislative mint with some intrinsic meaning. Sometimes it remains unchanged. Like currency, words sometimes appreciate or depreciate in value.

Frequently the sense of a word cannot be got except by fashioning a mosaic of significance out of the innuendoes of disjointed bits of statute. Cardozo phrased this familiar phenomenon by stating that "the meaning of a statute is to be looked for, not in any single section, but in all the parts together and in their relation to the end in view." [12] And to quote Cardozo once more on this phase of our problem: "There is need to keep in view also the structure of the statute, and the relation, physical and logical, between its several parts." [13]

The generating consideration is that legislation is more than composition. It is an active instrument of government which, for purposes of interpretation, means that laws have ends to be achieved. It is in this connection that Holmes said "Words are flexible." [14] Again it was Holmes, the last judge to give quarter to loose thinking or vague yearning, who said that "the general purpose is a more important aid to the meaning than any rule which grammar or formal logic may lay down." [15] And it was Holmes who chided courts for being "apt to err by sticking too closely to the words of a law where those words import a policy that goes beyond them." [16] Note, however, that he found the policy in "those words"!

"PROLIFERATION OF PURPOSE"

You may have observed that I have not yet used the word "intention." All these years I have avoided speaking of the "legislative intent" and I shall continue to be on my guard against using it. The objection to "intention" was indicated in a letter by Mr. Justice Holmes which the recipient kindly put at my disposal:

Only a day or two ago—when counsel talked of the intention of a legislature, I was indiscreet enough to say I don't care what their intention was. I only want to know what the words mean. Of course the phrase often is used to express a conviction not exactly thought out—that you construe a particular clause or expression by considering the whole instrument and any dominant purposes that it may express. In fact intention is a residuary clause intended to gather up whatever other aids there may be to interpretation beside the particular words and the dictionary.

If that is what the term means, it is better to use a less beclouding characterization. Legislation has an aim; it seeks to obviate some mischief, to supply an inadequacy, to effect a change of policy, to formulate a plan of government. That aim, that policy is not drawn, like nitrogen, out of the air; it is evinced in the language of the statute, as read in the light of other external manifestations of purpose. That is what the judge must seek and effectuate, and he ought not be led off the trail by tests that have overtones of subjective design. We are not concerned with anything subjective. We do not delve into the mind of legislators or their draftsmen, or committee members. Against what he believed to be such an attempt Cardozo once protested:

> The judgment of the court, if I interpret the reasoning aright, does not rest upon a ruling that Congress would have gone beyond its power if the purpose that it professed was the purpose truly cherished. The judgment of the court rests upon the ruling that another purpose, not professed, may be read beneath the surface, and by the purpose so imputed the statute is destroyed. Thus the process of psychoanalysis has spread to unaccustomed fields. There is a wise and ancient doctrine that a court will not inquire into the motives of a legislative body. . . .[17]

The difficulty in many instances where a problem of meaning arises is that the enactment was not directed towards the troubling question. The problem might then be stated, as once it was by Mr. Justice Cardozo, "which choice is it the more likely that Congress would have made?" [18] While in its context the significance and limitations of this question are clear, thus to frame the question too often tempts inquiry into the subjective and might seem to warrant the court in giving answers based on an unmanifested legislative state of mind. But the purpose which a court must effectuate is not that which Congress should have enacted, or would have. It is that which it did enact, however inaptly, because it may fairly be said to be imbedded in the statute, even if a specific manifestation was not thought of, as is often the very reason for casting a statute in very general terms.

Often the purpose or policy that controls is not directly revealed in the particular enactment. Statutes cannot be read intelligently if the eye is closed to considerations evidenced in affiliated statutes, or in the known temper of legislative opinion. Thus, for example, it is not lightly to be presumed that Congress sought to infringe on "very sacred rights." [19] This improbability will be a factor in determining whether language, though it should be so read if standing alone, was used to effect such a drastic change.

More frequently still it becomes important to remember, as in recent regulatory statutes, that the judicial task in marking out the extent to which Congress has exercised its constitutional power over commerce, is not that of devising an abstract formula. The task is one of accommodation as between assertions of new federal authority and historic functions of the individual States. Federal legislation of this character cannot therefore be construed without regard to the implications of our dual system of government. In such cases, for example, it is not to be assumed as a matter of course that when Congress adopts a new scheme for federal industrial regulation, it deals with all situations falling within the general mischief which gave rise to the legislation. The underlying assumptions of our dual form of government, and the consequent presuppositions of legislative draftsmanship which are expressive of our history and habits, cut across what might otherwise be the implied range of legislation. The history of congressional legislation regulating not only interstate commerce as such but also activities intertwined with it, justify the generalization that, when the federal government takes over such local radiations in the vast network of our national economic enterprise and thereby radically readjusts the balance of State and national authority, those charged with the duty of legislating are reasonably explicit and do not entrust its attainment to that restrospective expansion of meaning which properly deserves the stigma of judicial legislation.

SEARCH FOR PURPOSE

How then does the purpose which a statute expresses reveal itself, particularly when the path of purpose is not straight and narrow? The English courts say: look at the statute and look at nothing else. . . . [As Lord Haldane said in a 1922 decision,] "In *Millar* v. *Taylor* the principle of construction was laid down in words, which have never, so far as I know, been seriously challenged, by Willes J. as long ago as in 1769: 'The sense and meaning of an Act of Parliament must be collected from what it says when passed into a law; and not from the history of changes it underwent in the house where it took its rise. That history is not known to the other house or to the sovereign.' "

These current English rules of construction are simple. They are too simple. If the purpose of construction is the ascertainment of meaning, nothing that is logically relevant should be excluded.

The rigidity of English courts in interpreting language merely by reading it disregards the fact that enactments are, as it were, organisms which exist in their environment. One wonders whether English judges are confined psychologically as they purport to be legally. The judges deem themselves limited to reading the words of a statute. But can they really escape placing the words in the context of their minds, which after all are not automata applying legal logic but repositories of all sorts of assumptions and impressions? Such a modest if not mechanical view of the task of construction disregards legal history. In earlier centuries the judges recognized that the exercise of their judicial function to understand and apply legislative policy is not to be hindered by artificial canons and limitations. . . .

At the beginning, the Supreme Court reflected the early English attitude. With characteristic hardheadedness Chief Justice Marshall struck at the core of the matter with the observation "Where the mind labours to discover the design of the legislature, it seizes everything from which aid can be derived."[20] This commonsensical way of dealing with statutes fell into disuse, and more or less catchpenny canons of construction did service instead. To no small degree the vogue of a more wooden treatment of legislation arose, I suspect, because the need for keeping vividly in mind the occasions for drawing on all aids in the process of distilling meaning from legislation was comparatively limited. As the area of regulation steadily widened, the impact of the legislative process upon the judicial brought into being, and compelled consideration of, all that convincingly illumines an enactment, instead of merely that which is called, with delusive simplicity, "the end result." Legislatures themselves provided illumination by general definitions, special definitions, explicit recitals of policy, and even directions of attitudes appropriate for judicial construction. Legislative reports were increasingly drawn upon, statements by those in charge of legislation, reports of investigating committees, recommendations of agencies entrusted with the enforcement of laws, etc. etc. When Mr. Justice Holmes came to the Court, the United States Reports were practically barren of references to legislative materials. These swarm in current volumes. And let me say in passing that the importance that such materials play in Supreme Court litigation carry far-reaching implications for bench and bar.

The change I have summarized was gradual. Hesitations were felt and doubts were expressed even after the Court broke out of the mere language of a law. We find Mr. Justice Holmes saying, "It is a delicate business to base speculations about the purposes or construction of a statute upon the vicissitudes of its passage." [21] And as late as 1925 he referred to earlier bills relating to a statute under review, with the reservation "If it be legitimate to look at them." [22]

Such hesitations and restraints are in limbo. Courts examine the forms rejected in favor of the words chosen. They look at later statutes "considered to throw a cross light" upon an earlier enactment.[23] The consistent construction by an administrative agency charged with effectuating the policy of an enactment carries very considerable weight. While assertion of authority does not demonstrate its existence, long-continued, uncontested assertion is at least evidence that the legislature conveyed the authority. Similarly, while authority conferred does not atrophy by disuse, failure over an extended period to exercise it is some proof that it was not given. And since "a page of history is worth a volume of logic," [24] courts have looked into the background of statutes, the mischief to be checked and the good that was designed, looking sometimes far afield and taking notice also as judges of what is generally known by men.

Unhappily, there is no table of logarithms for statutory construction. No item of evidence has a fixed or even average weight. One or another may be decisive in one set of circumstances, while of little value elsewhere. A painstaking, detailed report by a Senate Committee bearing directly on the immediate question may settle the matter. A loose statement even by a chairman of a committee, made impromptu in the heat of debate, less informing in cold type than when heard on the floor, will hardly be accorded the weight of an encyclical.

Spurious use of legislative history must not swallow the legislation so as to give point to the quip that only when legislative history is doubtful do you go to the statute. While courts are no longer confined to the language, they are still confined by it. Violence must not be done to the words chosen by the legislature. Unless indeed no doubt can be left that the legislature has in fact used a private code, so that what appears to be violence to language is merely respect to special usage

In the end, language and external aids, each accorded the authority deserved in the circumstances, must be weighed in the balance of judicial judgment. Only if its premises are emptied of their human variables, can the process of statutory construction have the precision of a syllogism. We cannot avoid what Mr. Justice Cardozo deemed inherent in the problem of construction, making "a choice between uncertainties. We must be content to choose the lesser." [25] But to the discerning and disinterested eye, the scales will hardly escape appearing to tip slightly on the side of a more probable meaning.

"CANONS OF CONSTRUCTION"

Nor can canons of construction save us from the anguish of judgment. Such canons give an air of abstract intellectual compulsion to what is in fact a delicate judgment, concluding a complicated process of balancing subtle and elusive elements. All our three Justices have at one time or another leaned on the crutch of a canon. But they have done so only rarely, and with a recognition that these rules of construction are not in any true sense rules of law. So far as valid, they are what Mr. Justice Holmes called them, axioms of experience.[26] In many instances, these canons originated as observations in specific cases from which they were abstracted, taken out of the context of actuality, and, as it were, codified in treatises. . . .

Insofar as canons of construction are generalizations of experience, they all have worth. In the abstract, they rarely arouse controversy. Difficulties emerge when canons compete in soliciting judgment, because they conflict rather than converge. For the demands of judgment underlying the art of interpretation, there is no vade-mecum.

But even generalized restatements from time to time may not be wholly wasteful. Out of them may come a sharper rephrasing of the conscious factors of interpretation; new instances may make them more vivid but also disclose more clearly their limitations. Thereby we may avoid rigidities which, while they afford more precise formulas, do so at the price of cramping the life of law. To strip the task of judicial reading of statutes of rules that partake of the mysteries of a craft serves to reveal the true elements of our problem. It defines more accurately the nature of the intellectual responsibility of a judge and thereby subjects him to more relevant criteria of criticism. Rigorous analysis also sharpens the respective duties of legislature and courts in relation to the making of laws and to their enforcement.

FAIR CONSTRUCTION AND FIT LEGISLATION

The quality of legislative organization and procedure is inevitably reflected in the quality of legislative draftsmanship. Representative Monroney told the House last July that "95 percent of all the legislation that becomes law passes the Congress in the shape that it came from our committees. Therefore if our committee work is sloppy, if it is bad, if it is inadequate, our legislation in 95 percent of the cases will be bad and inadequate as well." And Representative Lane added that "In the second session of the 78th Congress 953 bills and resolutions were passed, of which only 86 were subject to any real discussion." [27] But what courts do with legislation may in turn deeply affect what Congress will do in the future. Emerson says somewhere that mankind is as lazy as it dares to be. Loose judicial reading makes for loose legislative writing. It encourages the practise illustrated in a recent cartoon in which a senator tells his colleagues "I admit this new bill is too complicated to understand. We'll just have to pass it to find out what it means." A modern Pascal might be tempted at times to say of legislation what Pascal said of students of theology when he charged them with "a looseness of thought and language that would pass nowhere else in making what are professedly very fine distinctions." And it is conceivable that he might go on and speak, as did Pascal, of the "insincerity with which terms are carefully chosen to cover opposite meanings." [28]

But there are more fundamental objections to loose judicial reading. In a democracy the legislative impulse and its expression should come from those popularly chosen to legislate and equipped to devise policy, as courts are not. The pressure on legislatures to discharge their responsibility with care, understanding and imagination should be stiffened, not relaxed. Above all, they must not be encouraged in irresponsible or undisciplined use of language. In the keeping of legislatures perhaps more than in that of any other group is the well-being of their fellow-men. Their responsibility is discharged ultimately by words. They are under a special duty therefore to observe that "Exactness in the use of words is the basis of all serious thinking. You will get nowhere without it. Words are clumsy tools, and it is very easy to cut one's fingers with them, and they need the closest attention in handling; but they are the only tools we have, and imagination itself cannot work without them. You must master the use of them, or you will wander forever guessing at the mercy of mere impulse and unrecognized assumptions and arbitrary associations, carried away with every wind of doctrine." [29]

Perfection of draftsmanship is as unattainable as demonstrable correctness of judicial reading of legislation. Fit legislation and fair adjudication are attainable. The ultimate reliance of society for the proper fulfillment of both these august functions is to entrust them only to those who are equal to their demands.

REFERENCES

[1] Mr. Justice Brandeis in *United States* v. *Moreland*, 258 U. S. 433, 451.

[2] *Carter* v. *Carter Coal Co.*, 298 U. S. 238, 327.

[3] See Sir Ernest Barker's Introduction to his translation of Aristotle's *Politics*, p. lxiii.

[4] *Hoeper* v. *Tax Commission*, 284 U. S. 206, 219.

[5] *Anderson* v. *Wilson*, 289 U. S. 20, 27.

[6] *Iselin* v. *United States*, 270 U. S. 245, 250-51.

[7] *St. Louis-San Francisco Ry.* v. *Middlekamp*, 256 U. S. 226, 232.

[8] *Boston Sand Co.* v. *United States*, 278 U. S. 41, 48.

[9] Cardozo, *Duparquet Co.* v. *Evans*, 297 U. S. 216, 220-21.

[10] *Henry* v. *United States*, 251 U. S. 393, 395.

[11] *Missouri* v. *Holland*, 252 U. S. 416, 433.

[12] *Panama Refining Co.* v. *Ryan*, 293 U. S. 388, 433, 439.

[13] *Duparquet Co.* v. *Evans*, 297 U. S. 216, 218.

[14] *International Stevedoring Co.* v. *Haverty*, 272 U. S. 50, 58.

[15] *United States* v. *Whitridge*, 197 U. S. 135, 143.

[16] *Olmstead* v. *United States*, 277 U. S. 438, 469.

[17] *United States* v. *Constantine*, 296 U. S. 287 at 298-99.

[18] *Burnet* v. *Guggenheim*, 288 U. S. 280, 285.

[19] *Milwaukee Publishing Co.* v. *Burleson*, 255 U. S. 407, 438.

[20] *United States* v. *Fisher*, 2 Cranch 358, 386.

[21] *Pine Hill Co.* v. *United States*, 259 U. S. 191, 196.

[22] *Davis* v. *Pringle*, 268 U. S. 315, 318.

[23] See *United States* v. *Aluminum Co. of America*, 148 F. 2d. 416, 429.

[24] *N. Y. Trust Co.* v. *Eisner*, 256 U. S. 345, 349.

[25] *Burnet* v. *Guggenheim*, 288 U. S. 280, 288.

[26] See *Boston Sand Co.* v. *United States*, 278 U. S. 41, 48.

[27] See 92 Congressional Record, pp. 10040 and 10054, July 25, 1946.

[28] See Pater, *Miscellaneous Studies*, Essay on Pascal, pp. 48, 51.

[29] See J. W. Allen's Essay on Jeremy Bentham, in *The Social and Political Ideas of the Revolutionary Era* (ed. by Hearnshaw), pp. 181, 199.

OWEN J. ROBERTS

ASSOCIATE JUSTICE, 1930-1945

Protecting the Court's Independence*

I feel entirely free to talk on this subject now because I have no longer any connection with any of the courts of the United States. I elected to resign the commission that I held and I am, like you, a common citizen and able, thank God, to express my view on public questions without feeling that I may, in some way, breach the proprieties. I cannot, of course, divorce myself from my experiences as a justice of the Supreme Court and I cannot divorce myself from the opinions that I formed then with respect to policies.

It is because I have been with that body and it is because I have a deep affection for the Court and a deep desire that it be protected and that it carry its place in our tri-une form of government [that I speak out on the following proposals now being discussed by the bar and the public.] . . .

The first proposal is that the Constitution should be amended to provide that the Supreme Court shall be composed of the Chief Justice of the United States and eight associate justices. It was a matter of remark by James Bryce that the personnel of the Supreme Court had changed so often in the history of the country. He did not quite understand it, that the number had run all the way from six to nine, up and back again. Of course, we understand there is nothing in the world to prevent the Court from being twenty if Congress should so legislate.

* From a speech before the Association of the Bar of the City of New York, New York, N. Y., December 11, 1948. Printed as "Now Is the Time: Fortifying the Supreme Court's Independence," 35 *American Bar Association Journal*, 1-4 (1949). Reprinted by permission of Mrs. Owen J. Roberts, W. H. Lathrop, and the publisher.

You will remember the great letter that Chief Justice Hughes wrote to the Congress in 1937, when the plan to increase the personnel of the Court was under consideration. He said justly then, as I think, that a court of nine is as large a court as is manageable. The Court could do its work, except for writing of the opinions, a good deal better if it were five rather than nine. Every man who is added to the Court adds another voice in council, and the most difficult work of the Court, as you may well have imagined, is that that is done around the council table; and if you make the Court a convention instead of a small body of experts, you will simply confuse council. It will confuse council within the Court, and will cloud the work of the Court and deteriorate and degenerate it. I have not any doubt about that.

The remedy for the weight of work that is placed on the Court is to increase the discretionary jurisdiction and not to increase the personnel of the Court. I can well understand how the founding fathers left the number at large because there were many problems that they could not envisage when they drafted the Constitution, and one of its great virtues is that it is drawn with a wide sweep and with a broad brush, and that details are left to be filled in afterwards. And that is one objection that will be made to these amendments of which I will speak in a minute.

The second proposal is an amendment to the Constitution that the Chief Justice of the United States and each associate justice of the Supreme Court shall retire when he shall attain the age of seventy-five years. I think little need be said about it. I believe it is a wise provision. First of all, it will forestall the basis of the last attack on the Court, the extreme age of the justices, and the fact that superannuated old gentlemen hung on there long after their usefulness had ceased. More than that, it tends to provide for each administration an opportunity to add new personnel to the Court, which, I think, is a good thing. I think it is a bad thing for an administration to run as long as President Roosevelt's did without a single opportunity to name a justice to the Court.

The third proposal has to do with the appellate jurisdiction of the Court, and I want to pass that for a moment, because that is the crux of what I have to say here today. . . . So I pass the third proposal for the moment and come to the fourth. The substance of it is that no person who hereafter shall become Chief Justice or an associate justice of the Supreme Court shall be eligible to the office of President or Vice President.

Just by so much as the Supreme Court is set apart, just because of the great powers the Supreme Court exercises in our constitutional system, there ought not to be any ambition in any man who sits in that Court to go beyond where he is. I would go farther than that. As a matter of personal belief, I do not think an associate justice ought to be eligible to be Chief Justice, and I do not think that any member of the Court ought to be eligible to hold any political office, but perhaps the present proposal goes far enough. It says that no justice shall be eligible to be President or Vice President.

It is a fact, as I think you know, that every justice who has ever sat on that Court who was bitten by political ambition and has actively promoted his own candidacy for office has hurt his own career as a judge and has hurt the Court. Instances run pretty far back in the history of the Court.

When a man goes on the Court he ought not to have to depend upon the strength and robustness of his own character to resist the temptation to shade a sentence in an opinion or to shade a view in order to put an umbrella up in case it should rain. He ought to be free to say his say, knowing, as the founding fathers meant he should know, that nothing could reach him and that his conscience was as free as could be.

The other limitations that the Constitution put, the good behavior clause, and the fact that a judge's compensation cannot be reduced during his term of office, were intended to guarantee him utter independence. He ought not to have to make a vow to himself that ambition shall not color his opinions. It should be impossible for that to happen.

Another proposal is that the Chief Justice or any associate justice or any judge of any other court of the United States shall not, *during his term of office*, hold any other governmental or public office or position.

A bill providing something of that sort was introduced in the last Congress. I feel very strongly that that would be a great protection to the Court. Perhaps it is enough protection to embody it in an act of Congress. It may be a little out of part for me to speak on this subject, for, as you know, I accepted, at the hands of two Presidents, commissions to do work not strictly of a judicial nature. I have every reason to regret that I ever did so. I do not think it was good for my position as a justice, nor do I think it was a good thing for the Court.

I had an unfortunate experience in the German-American Mixed Claims Commission, in which the German Commissioner accused me of bias and unfairness and walked out of the arbitration. I had another unpleasant experience as a result of the Pearl Harbor Commission report, when a Congressional investigating committee sought to comb over what was done, and there might have been rather an unfortunate reflection on the justice who was a member of that commission.

In the last administration, the Roosevelt administration, it got to be a very common thing to call on federal judges, not only of the Supreme Court but from other federal courts, to take part in administrative work. I think that is a bad thing for the courts, and I think it is not a good thing for the standing of the judges.

Of course, there is the question of how far you are going in amending the Constitution of the United States. I am all for the view that it ought to be a document stating great principles and not attempting the meticulousness of a regulatory statute. Every time you suggest an amendment, you violate, to some extent, that great principle.

I want to say that in my opinion this prohibition should extend not only to the Supreme Court but to all of the federal courts. If any of the federal judges have time to run around on all sorts of administrative work, then we have too many federal judges.

When I went to Pearl Harbor for three weeks I was out of the arguments and consultations in my Court. Chief Justice Stone agreed to my going with the greatest reluctance because he said: "There are some important cases coming up here, and I do not want a court of eight to hear them. A full court ought to hear them." But, as I say, he regretfully gave his consent as the President wanted me to go.

I agreed to take the Chairmanship of the German-American Mixed Claims Commission with the understanding that it would be but a few hours' work. It was years of work. It took time off from my judicial duties.

The last time that Chief Justice Hughes took a position of this kind, which was that of an international arbitrator between two South American countries, he said to me: "I will never do that

sort of thing again. It is not fair to the Court for one of us to
take time from the Court's work."

Some people think that if those proposals were adopted, the
independence and integrity of the Court would be well protected.
Others, and I am one of them, think that this does not go nearly
far enough. Now why?

Well, the third proposal to which I said I would return, suggests
an amendment of the judiciary article of the Constitution which
would give the Supreme Court appellate jurisdiction in all cases
arising under the Constitution, and give it appellate jurisdiction
both as to matters of law and matters of fact.

That is a major amendment of the authority of the Supreme
Court. It is a major enlargement of it. It is interesting that the
founding fathers fixed a very narrow obligatory jurisdiction, and
a jurisdiction that could not be touched or taken away, that
affecting ambassadors, other public ministers and suits in which
states would be a party.

Why did they then leave it to Congress to regulate the appellate jurisdiction of the Court? I think they did not envisage
any such large federal judiciary as we have today. The federal
judiciary was rather in the background—that is, the lower judiciary. The theory was that constitutional questions would arise
in state courts and then an appeal would come to the Supreme
Court from a decision of a state court on a constitutional question.

There came into play state pride, the states' rights feeling, and
another feeling that since Anglo-Saxons prize the jury system,
giving the Supreme Court appellate jurisdiction as to matters of
law and fact would give it the opportunity to overturn jury
verdicts, jury decisions, judgments based on jury decisions in New
York, in Pennsylvania and elsewhere. The best compromise that
could be made in the situation was to leave to Congress the right
to define the appellate jurisdiction of the Supreme Court.

You know what the result of that has been. The appellate
jurisdiction of the Supreme Court depends upon the judiciary
acts—the original Judiciary Act passed in the first session of
Congress and the amendments that have been adopted to it
since—and Congress has set forth in what cases the Supreme
Court can entertain an appeal.

Very early the Court was faced with the question whether it

had a general appellate jurisdiction, modified by what Congress had said on the subject. Chief Justice Marshall, in two decisions, said that was not the way to read the Constitution. He said that the Congress and the judiciary acts, having set forth in which cases the Supreme Court might have jurisdiction on appeal, impliedly provided that it should not take jurisdiction in any other class of cases.

That is the settled law and I think it is right. It remains, therefore, so far as we can see, that Congress could affect the Court's powers, just as President Roosevelt could have in his way, unless there were a popular uprising that would frighten them out of doing what they threatened to do.

You have, of course, in mind *Ex parte McCardle.* There was a case that had come up under the jurisdiction then existing under the judiciary acts. The case had been briefed, argued and submitted and was ready for a decision, when the Congress removed the appellate jurisdiction of the Supreme Court in that specific class of case. The Chief Justice wrote a short opinion in which he said that the jurisdiction was subject to regulation by Congress and that the Court had lost the power to deal with that case. The case was dismissed for want of jurisdiction.

That has never been done again. Nothing like it has ever been attempted, but it was done for political reasons and in a political exigency to meet a supposed emergency. The Court might well have said that, jurisdiction having existed when the case was submitted and the case now being in the bosom of the Court, it was too late for Congress to take away its jurisdiction; but you know how deferential the Court has been to the doctrine of the division of powers and evidently it was felt that that would be a straining of the Court's authority and that it should not do it. So it submitted to having its jurisdiction taken away after the case was ready for decision.

It is difficult to say that Congress could not reach the same result by a rather indirect route. Following the precedent that existed when the Emergency Court of Appeals was created to deal with OPA questions, Congress, it seems to me under the present phraseology of the Constitution, could create a federal court to hear certain classes of questions and provide that its decisions should be final.

Such a court might have to decide very serious constitutional questions, as the Emergency Court of Appeals had to do, and yet, if the Congress provided that its decision should be final and binding on the parties, and without appeal, what is there in the Constitution to prevent it? What is there to prevent Congress taking away, bit by bit, all the appellate jurisdiction of the Supreme Court of the United States, not doing it by direct attack but by that sort of indirect attack?

I see nothing. I do not see any reason why Congress cannot, if it elects to do so, take away entirely the appellate jurisdiction of the Supreme Court of the United States over state supreme court decisions. The jurisdiction is exercised now under the terms of the Judiciary Act. Suppose Congress should decide to let the decisions of state courts of appeal be final on constitutional questions. How could the Supreme Court assert a power to take those questions, notwithstanding the act of Congress, in view of the language of the Third Article of the Constitution?

That is the real loophole. What is the use of talking about limiting and fixing the number of the justices so that the Court cannot be packed; what is the utility of saying that the justices must retire at a certain period so as not to have an old, tired, superannuated Court; what is the good of providing that we shall make the Court less conscious of the political movements in the country by depriving the justices of the right to have any ambition for future office; if you leave the Court's appellate powers open to be dealt with and be set aside by action of Congress in any given class of cases or in all the cases which, traditionally, it has dealt with as the final appellate body under the Constitution?

For some reason or other this proposal has met with more opposition than the others. In my opinion, without it you have made a bucket and left a hole through which the bucket can empty itself. In other words, this carefully envisaged plan to protect the judiciary would be left with a defect which renders the protective measures futile.

I want to speak a moment about the objections that have been presented. The opposition says that the whole project of amending the judiciary article of the Constitution is to be frowned upon; that we ought not to tinker with our fundamental law; that we have lived under this Judiciary Act for these 160 years; that we have gotten along pretty well; and that it is reasonable to suppose we would get along in the future.

They take the position, on the other hand, that it is a pretty good thing the Constitution left this hole in it so that the Congress can act as a safety valve if the Court gets too heady.

The arguments are rather inconsistent. The one says "Don't touch the Constitution." The other says "It has a great big hole in it. Nobody has run through the hole yet, and let's take a chance that nobody ever will."

They argue that it would be futile to adopt these amendments. They say that if the people rise and attempt to destroy the Court, it will not matter what the Constitution says about the powers of the Court. But what we are trying to provide against is not an overthrow of the Constitution but a tinkering with the Court by legislative or administrative action without violating the letter of the Constitution.

If we have a revolution and the constitutional system under which we live is destroyed by main force, it will not matter what the Constitution provides. But those who are supporting these amendments are supporting them in the belief that the general framework of our constitutional government is to be perpetuated and they want that framework of government to go on along the lines that traditionally we have been led to understand were the divisional lines between the executive, the judicial and the legislative.

Then, finally, there has been a suggestion that the Court ought not to be strengthened because the Court, as presently constituted, does not have the entire respect of the Bar. This I think a desperately bad argument. The Court is a great institution. Just because you and I may not like its decisions today, why should we encourage an opportunity to a politician some time to reach in and change its personnel, or change its jurisdiction? I do not think it is a worthy argument.

The Court could, in effect, be destroyed by a President's appointing consistently desperately bad men to it. But are we to indulge a fear of that? I think not.

That is a summary of the opposition, as I understand it, and I do not think the arguments are valid. I do not see why we should not write into the judiciary article what right-thinking citizens and the Bar have felt is the tradition of the Court and is the core of the Court's fulfilling its independent functions in our system of government I do not see any reason why we should fear to stand up for our views in this respect because it is a bad thing to get into discussions about constitutional amendments and about our system, and that it is only putting bad ideas into people's heads. We would never have any progress if we were afraid to stand up for what we think right.

We have seen what the dangers are that have popped up now and again, in *Ex parte McCardle* and in the last administration in two or three aspects. It is just good housekeeping and just good insurance and just good common sense to put into the Constitution explicitly what you and I all think has been there by tradition for a long time and which ought not to be subject to change.

So, while I am generally against tinkering with the Constitution, I am for making the judiciary branch as safe from attack as the founding fathers evidently expected and desired it should be, and I think the proposed amendments taken together will do that effectively, and that nothing short of them will do it.

WILLIAM J. BRENNAN, JR.

ASSOCIATE JUSTICE, 1956—

State Court Decisions and the Supreme Court*

. . . The work of the Supreme Court, especially significant, as, of course, it is, must not divert attention from the vital importance of the work of the state courts in the administration of justice. Actually the composite work of the courts of the 50 States probably has greater significance in measuring how well America attains the ideal of equal justice for all. We emphasize this when we remind ourselves that the Supreme Court is intruded between the state courts and litigants in a very narrow class of litigation. That, of course, is the class of cases in which the state courts deal with federal questions. This intrusion is required because the Supreme Court has been assigned the unique responsibility for umpiring our federal system. That role has always been and remains the Court's most important function. The role was devised that we might realize as a people our dream of one Nation of 50 independent sovereignties. All the States must be held equally obedient to the same interpretation of the commands of the Constitution. If each were free to follow its own interpretation, Balkanization of the Nation into quarreling sections or regions would inevitably follow. It is state judicial decisions turning on constitutional or other federal questions to which the Supreme Court, therefore, must attend. Some of those cases raise questions of the applicability of the Supremacy Clause or other conflicts between state and federal power, a few arise in state litigation under federal statutes, but most often the

* From speech to the Pennsylvania Bar Association, Pittsburgh, Pa., February 3, 1960. Printed in 31 *Penna. Bar Association Quarterly* 393 (1960). Reprinted by permission of Mr. Justice Brennan and the publisher.

cases present challenges to state action under the Fourteenth Amendment. For some 90 years, in consequence of the adoption of that Amendment, every enactment of every State, every action by the Governor of a State, any governmental act of any of the States, or of the instrumentalities thereof, including judicial actions, may in a proper case be challenged at the Bar of the Supreme Court on the ground that such action, such legislation, such state court decision, is a deprivation of liberty without due process of law, or denies the equal protection of the laws. I don't mean that the enforcement of constitutional limitations and guarantees is not also a responsibility of the state courts. To the contrary, the obligation rests upon the state courts, equally with the federal courts, to guard, enforce, and protect every right granted or secured by the Federal Constitution. The point is that the Supreme Court is concerned with state judicial determinations only because the distribution of judicial power under our federal system assigns the responsibility for ultimate constitutional interpretation as well as final decision of other federal questions to the Supreme Court.

It is important, however, to stress how infinitesimally small is the class of cases as to which the state courts may have to share judicial power with the Supreme Court because they raise federal questions. I suppose the state courts of all levels must decide annually literally millions of controversies which involve vital issues of life, liberty, and property of human beings of this Nation. Even the yearly total of decisions handed down by the highest courts of the 50 States must run into the tens of thousands. Yet only a dribble of this vast number raises any federal question. Last Term in only 792 state cases did losers knock on the Supreme Court's door and protest that a state court had erroneously decided a federal question. Nine out of 10 of even that scant number did not get in. We turned away 734 or 93%. We could find only 58 state court decisions of federal questions which justified our inquiry into the merits of the disposition of those questions by the state courts. We heard and decided 30 of those cases. We affirmed 13 of the state judgments and reversed 17. Contrast the 30 state cases argued and decided with the 75 cases from the federal courts which were argued and decided. We reviewed over twice as many federal court decisions. The state decisions reviewed were from the courts of 17 States. The highest number from any one state court was six; only a single case came from each of 10 States. . . .

Of course, there are almost always far-reaching results from our review of a state court decision. This is necessarily the case when the decision performs the umpire function of resolving a conflict between state and federal power or between state action and the Federal Constitution. Inevitably the disposition carries implications and gives directions beyond the fact of the particular case. True the same thing may often be said of a decision of a high state court. Many state court decisions, as we all know, have great influence in shaping the course of the law. But if the effect of a state court decision ordinarily is only within the State, almost never can the effect of a Supreme Court decision be contained within the borders of the State concerned. Consider state criminal convictions which the Supreme Court reviews. As a people Americans want stern application of the criminal law. But our Constitution commands that even the most obviously guilty shall be convicted for his crime only by processes measuring up to the standards of fairness and decency to which our civilized society strives to be true. Those standards have been largely articulated by the Supreme Court in cases brought to light in the usually crudely phrased and sometimes desperate pleas of those denied liberty, or perhaps about to forfeit life under a state judgment. The constitutional standards so developed become standards not for that case or State alone but for the administration of criminal justice in all the States.

For example, last Term we sustained Florida's version of the uniform law to secure the attendance of witnesses from within or without the State. That statute was attacked on the ground it offended the restrictions on state action of the Fourteenth Amendment. That uniform law has been adopted by most of the States. Again we sustained an Illinois conviction for bank robbery despite the prior acquittal of the accused for the federal offense committed by the same robbery. We upheld Oklahoma's death sentence for kidnapping although the kidnapper had already received a life sentence for the murder of his victim. We affirmed Louisiana's criminal contempt conviction of a grand jury witness who although granted full immunity from state prosecution refused to answer questions on the ground of possible federal incrimination under the federal income tax laws. We also sustained a criminal contempt conviction by the New York courts of a witness before an *in camera* judicial inquiry who refused to testify unless his lawyer was also allowed to be present. On the other side of the coin we reversed an Illinois robbery conviction because obtained on testimony known by the prosecutor to be perjured, a New York murder conviction obtained on a confession given involuntarily, Ohio's refusal of appellate review to a prisoner who could not pay the filing fee for an appeal, and, as violative of procedural due process, contempt convictions sustained by the Virginia and Ohio courts of witnesses who refused to answer questions before state legislative committees. Everyone of those decisions pronounced standards of general application to the States in the enforcement of their criminal laws.

And yet it is true that a federal question emerges from the grist of the state courts with greatest rarity. If cases were grains of sand, federal question cases would be hard to find on the beach. The final and vital decisions of most controversies upon which depend life, liberty, and property are made by the state courts. This, of course, is as it should be in a federal system where the first responsibility for the preservation of ordered liberty belongs to the States.

It is because the Supreme Court's review of state court decisions is limited to review of federal questions that a state judge coming to the Supreme Court learns that his state court experience has not always fully prepared him for his new work. Even the master, Holmes, shortly after coming from over 20 years on the Massachusetts Supreme Judicial Court, was to write Pollock that the new work was "an adventure into the unknown." The state court judge who has dealt primarily with problems of property, contract, fault, crime, and zoning finds that he must sharpen his familiarity with the different bench marks that direct his judgments in the Supreme Court.

But none should mistake the difference in the character of the problems as a difference in the exacting nature of the tasks performed by the judges of both courts. It is true that no other court may review judgments of the United States Supreme Court. That fact casts perhaps a special responsibility on the Supreme Court in the decisional process. This is what Mr. Justice Jackson had in mind when he admonished us: "We are not final because we are infallible, but we are infallible only because we are final."

If the responsibilities differ on that account this is at best a difference of degree, certainly it is not a difference in kind. The last Supreme Court judge from a state court to come to the United States Supreme Court before me, Benjamin Cardozo, saw the truth of the case. He expressed misgivings, you will remember, about leaving the New York Court of Appeals. He said: "Whether the new field of usefulness is greater I don't know. Perhaps the larger opportunity was where I have been."

I hope you will understand from what I have said to now why I find my present function in relation to a state court case very different from my function in state cases when I sat on the New Jersey Supreme Court. Perhaps the details as to our procedures when we are approached to review a state court decision will interest you. I need not tell this audience that the litigant seeking Supreme Court review of a state case usually invokes our discretionary certiorari jurisdiction. Only a few state cases qualify as appeals entitling the appealing party as a matter of right to have the Court exercise its jurisdiction and decide the case one way or another. Such cases are rare since an appeal of right from a state judgment is virtually limited to a final judgment which declares a federal statute unconstitutional, or a state statute valid in the face of a challenge on federal constitutional grounds.

Crucial to the exercise of our certiorari jurisdiction is whether the controlling issue in the state court case is a federal issue, that is, an issue arising under the United States Constitution or under federal laws or treaties. But the fact that a federal question lurks in the case doesn't mean, standing alone, that a state decision will be reviewed. *First*, the federal question must be a substantial question. *Second*, the federal question must have been properly raised in the state courts. This is required because the state courts must first be afforded an opportunity to consider and decide the federal question. *Third*, even then we may not take the case if the state court's judgment can be sustained on an independent ground of state law. But whether there is a substantial question and whether it was properly raised in the state courts and whether, even so, the state court decision can be rested on an independent state ground are not always easy questions. The parties differ on one or more of them and we of the Court are not always in agreement. Actually the applicant's most difficult task is to persuade at least four of us that his case qualifies for and warrants review. While, when nine of us sit, it takes five of us to decide a case on the merits, it takes only the votes of four to grant a review on the merits. But those four votes are hard to come by—only the exceptional state case raising a significant federal question commands them. . . .

Of the 792 state cases acted on last Term, I repeat that only 58 commanded the necessary four votes for review of the merits. You will inquire what is the status of the 734 which failed to get four votes. The answer is that the judgments of the state courts remain undisturbed. Now I said "undisturbed"—I did not say "affirmed." A denial of certiorari is not an affirmance of the state court judgment as some erroneously think. It means only the petition for review did not get four votes and it means absolutely nothing more.

The denial does not mean that the Court agrees with the result reached by the state court or with the state court's decision of the federal question. Very often I have voted to deny an application when I thought that the state court's result was very wrong. The six or more Justices voting to refuse review may and indeed, often do, differ upon the grounds of their common action. Some may conclude that the federal question raised was not substantial, others that it had not been properly raised in the state courts, others that in any event the state court decision rested on an independent state ground. Or some may have concluded that a case otherwise qualifying for review nevertheless raised an issue not appropriate at the time for review. Thus I emphasize a denial in nowise implies agreement with the state court's decision of the federal question even if that decision turned on that question. The Court may well take the very next case raising the same question and reach a different result on the merits. . . .

But the ultimate resolution of conflicts between state and federal power, and between the individual and governmental power asserted against him by either state or federal governments is the peculiar responsibility of the Supreme Court. The Founders created a federalism diffusing governmental power between national and state governments and imposing restrictions upon both designed to prevent oppression of the individual. But the Founders were not so optimistic as to think that paper delineations of power would be a sure and certain guarantee against excesses of its exercise. They were practical as well as wise men and were fully aware of the inevitability of conflicts as to what power belonged to which sovereignty and how far either sovereignty might interfere with the liberty of the citizen. Such are the limitations of the human mind, of human imagination, that no genius of constitution making could have delineated the precise boundaries of the powers assigned the several repositories of governmental power. Nor in the nature of things could the Framers have fashioned precise guide lines for the resolution of the myriad collisions between power exercised by any of these repositories and the guarantees of individual liberty erected to restrain governmental oppression whatever its source.

Some institution had to referee these conflicts and the Framers chose the Supreme Court ultimately to perform that duty. The guide lines are indistinct. This much however is clear: the economic and social conflicts of our history come ultimately to the Court for final resolution. Over a century and a half ago De Tocqueville perceptively observed that by the very nature of our Constitution practically every political question in time comes to the Court in the guise of a judicial question. Still our history has been that many a controversy that elsewhere is settled by the conquest of arms, is, eventually anyhow, settled by force of reason.

Let me return for a moment to the handful of cases where both the state courts and the Supreme Court function. Very obviously the correct analysis of their respective responsibilities for decision is not in terms of which has the greater and which the lesser burden. The responsibilities are of the same gravity. The difference lies merely in the fact that the Supreme Court has the final word on federal questions. One thing the judges of both courts do have in common. Both, like other human beings responsible for other human institutions, are on the dubious waves of error tossed. But in performing their respective tasks in cases where both must function there can be no reason for contest, not even for petty quarrel. For they have this, too, in common—that both are equally devoted, and conscientiously devoted, to the sincere and continuing effort to arrive at truth—at justice.

PART THREE

Precedent, Segregation, and "The Law"

"Our Constitution is a written instrument. The 14th amendment does not specifically mention public schools. Having decided unanimously that the legislative history was not conclusive that the Congress or the States intended it should apply to schools, one would think the Court would have stopped there and upheld the previous decisions of the Court. Instead, it proceeded to reverse those decisions and legislate a policy for schools. . . . Power intoxicates men. It is never voluntarily surrendered. It must be taken from them. The Supreme Court must be curbed.

Former Justice James F. Byrnes

"The place of *stare decisis* in constitutional law is . . . [highly] tenuous. A judge looking at a constitutional decision may have compulsions to revere past history and accept what was once written. But he remembers above all else that it is the Constitution which he swore to support and defend, not the gloss which his predecessors may have put on it. So he comes to formulate his own views, rejecting some earlier ones as false and embracing others. He cannot do otherwise unless he lets men long dead and unaware of the problems of the age in which he lives do his thinking for him."

Mr. Justice Douglas

"It is not by chance that a news columnist recently attacked law reviews and what he considered their improper influence on judicial decisions. The mind of the layman unfamiliar with the judicial process supposes it to exist in the air, as a self-justifying and wholly independent process. The opposite is of course true, that judicial decision must be nourished by all the insights that scholarship can furnish and legal scholarship must in turn be nourished by all the disciplines that comprehend the totality of human experience."

Mr. Justice Brennan

JAMES F. BYRNES

ASSOCIATE JUSTICE, 1941-1942

Usurpation by the Court*

Two years ago, on May 17, 1954, the Supreme Court of the United States reversed what had been the law of the land for 75 years and declared unconstitutional the laws of 17 States under which segregated public-school systems were established.

The Court did not interpret the Constitution—the Court amended it.

We have had a written Constitution. Under that Constitution the people of the United States have enjoyed great progress and freedom. The usurpation by the Court of the power to amend the Constitution and destroy State governments may impair our progress and take our freedom.

An immediate consequence of the segregation decision is that much of the progress made in the last half century of steadily advancing racial amity has been undone. Confidence and trust have been supplanted by suspicion and distrust. The races are divided and the breach is widening. The truth is, there has not been such tension between the races in the South since the days of reconstruction.

One threatened consequence is the closing of public schools in many States of the South.

A further consequence is the harm done to the entire country by the demonstrated willingness of the Supreme Court to disregard our written Constitution and its own decisions, invalidate the laws of States, and substitute for these a policy of its own, supported not by legal precedents but by the writings of sociologists.

Today, this usurpation by the Court of the power of the States

* From "The Supreme Court Must Be Curbed," *United States News and World Report* (published at Washington), May 18, 1956, pp. 50-58. Copyright 1956 United States Publishing Corporation. Reprinted with permission of the Honorable James F. Byrnes.

hurts the South. Tomorrow, it may hurt the North, East, and West. It may hurt you.

Though there was no dissenting opinion from any member of the Court, the South dissents. That dissent is reflected in State legislation and in the day-by-day occurrences throughout the South, developments which portray the feeling of the people. . . .

In 1896 in a case known as Plessy against Ferguson, involving a statute providing for segregation of the races on railroad trains, the United States Supreme Court held that a statute providing for separate but equal facilities was not in violation of the 14th amendment to the Constitution. Thereafter, the Supreme Court in several cases involving schools upheld this doctrine.

Later, the Court, when it included such great Judges as Chief Justice Taft and Justices Holmes, Brandeis, and Stone, unanimously said that segregation in public schools had been "many times decided to be within the constitutional power of the State legislatures to settle without interference of the Federal courts under the Federal Constitution."

SOUTH'S STAKE IN SEPARATE SCHOOLS

Relying upon the stability of the law of the land, and upon the guaranty of State sovereignty in the Federal Constitution, the people of the South invested hundreds of millions of dollars in separate schools for the races. Under this segregated school system, the southern Negro made greater progress than any other body of Negro people in the history of the world. . . .

About the time [a new] educational program [for more Negro schools] was inaugurated in South Carolina, there was pending in the U. S. court a case from Clarendon County, asking equal facilities for Negro schools. Later that suit was withdrawn, and a suit was brought by the same complainants asking the court to declare unconstitutional all segregation laws.

The three-judge court, presided over by Judge Parker, senior judge of the fourth circuit, held that under the decisions of the U. S. Supreme Court from 1896 to that date, the segregation provisions of the Constitution and statutes of South Carolina were not in violation of the 14th amendment. The lawyers for the National Association for the Advancement of Colored People appealed the case to the U. S. Supreme Court.

In that Court, the case for Clarendon County was argued by

the late Honorable John W. Davis. He was so convinced of the soundness of the decision of the three-judge court that he agreed to argue the case and declined to accept compensation for his services.

Had the Court been unanimous in the view that segregation statutes were in violation of the 14th amendment, such an opinion would have been written within a few months.

Instead, after many months, the Court announced that the cases should be reargued, and counsel should direct their argument to certain questions.

The first question was:

"What evidence is there that the Congress which submitted and the State legislatures and conventions which ratified the 14th amendment, contemplated or did not contemplate, understand or did not understand that it would abolish segregation in public schools?"

Such a question would not have been asked if a majority of the Court was already satisfied that Congress and the State legislatures did contemplate that the amendment would prohibit segregation in public schools.

Attorneys representing the parties involved and the attorneys general of many States having segregation statutes filed briefs. The overwhelming preponderance of the legislative history demonstrated that abolishing segregation in schools was not contemplated by the framers of the 14th amendment, or by the States.

We can only speculate as to how the Court reached its decision. . . .

The Court, in its opinion, did not admit . . . the conclusiveness of the evidence that the 14th amendment did not apply to school segregation. The Court said the evidence was inconclusive.

PREVIOUS DECISIONS WERE REVERSED

Our Constitution is a written instrument. The 14th amendment does not specifically mention public schools. Having decided unanimously that the legislative history was not conclusive that the Congress or the States intended it should apply to schools, one would think the Court would have stopped there and upheld the previous decisions of the Court. Instead, it proceeded to reverse those decisions and legislate a policy for schools. . . .

The Court, having previously interpreted the 14th amendment

to apply to jury service and other matters not specifically delegated by the Constitution to the Federal Government, felt that the soundness of those decisions would be questioned unless the Court held the 14th amendment to apply to schools.

But there was a distinction. Previously the Court had held that State laws providing separate but equal school facilities did not deny a constitutional right. The control of schools had been proposed by some framers of the 14th amendment and rejected. There was no legislation by Congress prohibiting segregated schools. The only change in conditions was that several million Negroes had migrated to the big cities in Northern States and constituted the balance of political power in several States.

Once the Court becomes committed to a course of expanding the Constitution in order to justify previous expansions, there is no turning back. When next the Court is called upon to "read into" the Constitution something which was never there, another segment of the people may be the victim. It may be you.

The Constitution provides that any amendment submitted to the States must be ratified by three-fourths of the States.

Change was purposely made difficult by the framers, who jealously guarded their liberties. They knew "the history of liberty is the history of limitations on government."

COURT IGNORED A WARNING

In amending the Constitution, the Court ignored the warning of George Washington in his Farewell Address:

"If, in the opinion of the people, the distribution or modification of the constitutional powers be in any particular wrong, let it be corrected by an amendment in the way which the Constitution designates. But let there be no change by usurpation; for though this, in one instance, may be the instrument of good, it is the customary weapon by which free governments are destroyed."

Frequently, the Court has applied a constitutional principle to subjects not specifically mentioned in the Constitution, and not conceived of by its framers. That has been done, for instance, in applying the "commerce clause" to congressional legislation affecting forms of transportation and communication not in existence when the "commerce clause" was adopted. Material progress, which could not have been anticipated, justified the Court in applying the principle of the "commerce clause" and sustaining the laws affecting commerce between the States.

Ordinarily, the Court has been controlled by legal precedents. In the segregation opinion, it could cite no legal precedent for its decision because all the precedents sustain the doctrine of separate but equal facilities.

In 23 of the States that ratified the 14th amendment, the courts of last resort held it did not abolish segregation. The Supreme Court itself, in 6 cases decided over a period of 75 years, upheld the doctrine of equal but separate facilities.

The Court ignored all of these legal precedents and the Constitution and said, "We cannot turn the clock back to 1868 when the amendment was adopted, or even to 1896 when *Plessy* v. *Ferguson* was written."

Why not? The function of the Court is to interpret the Constitution, not amend it. Heretofore, whenever in doubt about the proper interpretation of the Constitution or a statute, the Court has turned the clock back to the time of adoption to ascertain the intent of the draftsmen. When the Court states, "We cannot turn the clock back to 1868," will it ever consider the intent of the framers of the Constitution in 1787?

If the age of a constitutional provision is to be held against its soundness, what about the age of our religion? If time invalidates truth in one field, will it not do so in another?

If the Court could not turn the clock back in these cases, why did it ask counsel for the litigants and the attorneys general of all interested States to file briefs as to the intent of the Congress in 1868, in submitting, and the States, in ratifying, the amendments?

And why were counsel asked to argue whether the Court was bound by its previous decisions, such as *Plessy* v. *Ferguson?*

It is apparent that, when the Court found the legislative history it requested was overwhelming against the conclusion it had reached, it declared the evidence "inconclusive," disregarded the Constitution and—invading the legislative field—declared that segregation would retard the development of Negro children.

That was a terrible indictment of the Negro race. Because— whether a person be black, brown or yellow—whenever the Supreme Court says he cannot develop unless while in school he is permitted to sit by the side of the white students, the Court brands that person an inferior human being.

Now mark this well. The Court not only ignored the Constitution and its own decisions, but, in establishing a policy for schools, ignored the record in the case.

In support of its decision, after citing K. B. Clark, who was employed by the National Association for the Advancement of Colored People, it cited the writings of a group of psychologists who had not testified in the trial court. Counsel for the States had no opportunity to rebut the opinions of these psychologists. In such procedure there lies danger for all of us.

And the Court was guilty of what it has frequently condemned. As late as 1952 in the case of *Beauharnais* v. *Illinois* (343 U. S. 250), the Court said:

"It is not within our competence to confirm or deny claims of social scientists as to the dependence of the individual on the position of his racial or religious group in the community."

Counsel had no opportunity to cross-examine these psychologists as to their qualifications as well as their affiliations. However, in the U. S. Senate on May 26, 1955, Senator Eastland, chairman of the Senate Judiciary Committee, submitted an amazing record of several of the authorities cited by the Court. He said:

"Then, too, we find cited by the Court as another modern authority on psychology to override our Constitution, one Theodore Brameld, regarding whom the files of the Committee on Un-American Activities of the U. S. House of Representatives are replete with citations and information. He is cited as having been a member of no less than 10 organizations declared to be communistic, communistic-front, or Communist dominated."

As to E. Franklin Frazier, another authority cited by the Supreme Court, Senator Eastland said, "The files of the Committee on Un-American Activities of the U. S. House of Representatives contain 18 citations of Frazier's connections with Communist causes in the United States."

In support of its findings, the Court said, "See generally Myrdal, 'An American Dilemma, 1944.'" I have seen it. On page 13, Professor (Gunnar Karl) Myrdal writes that the Constitution of the United States is "impractical and unsuited to modern conditions" and its adoption was "nearly a plot against the common people."

On page 530, Myrdal states, "In the South the Negro's person and property are practically subject to the whim of any white person who wishes to take advantage of him or to punish him for any real or fancied wrongdoing or insult."

Millions of people, white and colored, know this is absolutely false. Members of the Supreme Court know it is false. It is an insult to the millions of white southerners.

Senator Eastland also listed some of those who were associated with Myrdal in writing his book. He stated that the files of the House Committee on Un-American Activities show that many of Myrdal's associates are members of organizations cited as subversive by the Department of Justice under Democratic and Republican administrations.

I am informed by the Senator that no Member of the Senate and no responsible person outside of the Senate has challenged the accuracy of his statements on this subject. Loyal Americans of the North, East, South, and West should be outraged that the Supreme Court would reverse the law of the land upon no authority other than some books written by a group of psychologists about whose qualifications we know little and about whose loyalty to the United States there is grave doubt.

And loyal Americans should stop and think when the executive branch of the Federal Government brands as subversive organizations whose membership includes certain psychologists, and the Supreme Court cites those psychologists as authority for invalidating the constitutions of 17 States of the Union.

RIGHT TO CRITICIZE COURT

Some advocates of integrated schools shudder to think of anyone's criticizing a decision of the Supreme Court or, certainly, this decision of the Court. Well, whenever a member of the Court dissents from the majority opinion, he expresses his views and criticizes—sometimes in vigorous language—the Court's opinion.

In recent years there are many examples. But a case in point is the dissent of the late Justice Owen J. Roberts, who differed with his colleagues on the Court in the case of *Smith* v. *Allwright*. The Supreme Court in that case reversed prior decisions and declared the Democratic Party in Texas was, in effect, an agency of the

State and that its actions (in conducting white primaries) was "State action." Said Mr. Justice Roberts:

"I have expressed my views with respect to the present policy of the Court freely to disregard and to overrule considered decisions and the rules of law announced in them. This tendency, it seems to me, indicates an intolerance for what those who have composed this Court in the past have conscientiously and deliberately concluded, and involves an assumption that knowledge and wisdom reside in us which was denied to our predecessors."

The decisions of the Supreme Court must be accepted by the courts of the United States and the States, but not necessarily by the court of public opinion. The people are not the creatures of the Court. The Court is the creature of the people.

One hundred representatives of the people in the U. S. Congress have issued a manifesto criticizing this decision. Such criticism is nothing new. There is precedent for criticism by the people.

After the decision in the Dred Scott case, Abraham Lincoln criticized the Court, declaring the decision erroneous and pledging the Republican Party to "do what we can to have it overruled."

President Franklin D. Roosevelt, on March 9, 1937, commenting on a decision of the Supreme Court, said:

"The Court in addition to the proper use of its judicial functions has improperly set itself up as a third house of the Congress —a superlegislature, as one of the Justices has called it—reading into the constitution words and implications which are not there.

"We have, therefore, reached the point as a Nation where we must take action to save the Constitution from the Court and the Court from itself.

"Our difficulty with the Court today rises not from the Court as an institution but from human beings within it." . . .

THREATENED: POWER OF STATES

Tragic as may be the consequences in destroying the public school system in the South, more frightening are the consequences of the trend of the present Court to destroy the powers of the 48 States.

In the case of *Pennsylvania* v. *Steve Nelson*, decided April 2, 1956, the same Court that declared unconstitutional the segregation statutes of 17 States invalidated the laws of 42 States prohibiting the knowing advocacy of the overthrow of the Government of the United States by violence, as long as there is a Federal law against sedition.

The Department of Justice protested to the Court that the State laws did not interfere with the enforcement of the Federal statute. But the Court struck down the laws of 42 States. Justices Reed, Burton, and Minton vigorously dissented.

One week later the Court declared unconstitutional a provision of the charter of New York City under which Professor Slochower, an employee, was dismissed for failure to answer a question in an authorized inquiry, on the ground that his answer might incriminate him. It is encouraging to the people that the same three Justices dissented and were joined by Justice Harlan.

Power intoxicates men. It is never voluntarily surrendered. It must be taken from them. The Supreme Court must be curbed.

The Constitution authorizes the Congress to regulate the appellate jurisdiction of the Supreme Court. Loyal Americans who believe in constitutional government appeal to the court of public opinion in the hope that you will urge the Congress to act before it is too late.

The present trend brings joy to Communists and their fellow travelers who want to see all power centered in the Federal Government because they can more easily influence one Government in Washington than the 48 governments in 48 States.

But the trend of the Court is disturbing to millions of Americans who respect the Constitution and believe that in order to preserve the Republic we must preserve what is left of the powers of the States.

You may be unconcerned today. You may cry tomorrow.

WILLIAM O. DOUGLAS

ASSOCIATE JUSTICE, 1939—

Stare Decisis[*]

. . . We live in an age of doubt and confusion. Rules that once seemed fixed and certain today seem beclouded. Principles of law have been challenged and judges asked to refashion them. Many raised their voices in protest. Some were special pleaders with a stake in existing law. Others had a sincere belief that the foremost function of law in these days of stress and strain is to remain steady and stable so as to promote security. Thus judges have been admonished to hold steadfast to ancient precedents lest the courts themselves add fresh doubt, confusion, and concern over the strength of our institutions.

This search for a static security—in the law or elsewhere—is misguided. The fact is that security can only be achieved through constant change, through the wise discarding of old ideas that have outlived their usefulness, and through the adapting of others to current facts. There is only an illusion of safety in a Maginot Line. Social forces like armies can sweep around a fixed position and make it untenable. A position that can be shifted to meet such forces and at least partly absorb them alone gives hope of security.

I speak here of long-term swings in the law. I do not suggest that *stare decisis* is so fragile a thing as to bow before every wind. The law is not properly susceptible to whim or caprice. It must have the sturdy qualities required of every framework that is designed for substantial structures. Moreover, it must have uniformity when applied to the daily affairs of men.

[*] (Let the decision stand.) From the Eighth Benjamin N. Cardozo Lecture delivered before the Association of the Bar of the City of New York, New York, N. Y., April 12, 1949. Published in *The Record* of the Association, Vol. 4 (1949), pp. 152-179. Reprinted by permission of Mr. Justice Douglas and the publisher. Footnotes renumbered.

Uniformity and continuity in law are necessary to many activities. If they are not present, the integrity of contracts, wills, conveyances and securities is impaired.[1] And there will be no equal justice under law if a negligence rule is applied in the morning but not in the afternoon. *Stare decisis* provides some moorings so that men may trade and arrange their affairs with confidence. *Stare decisis* serves to take the capricious element out of law and to give stability to a society. It is a strong tie which the future has to the past.

It is easy, however, to overemphasize *stare decisis* as a principle in the lives of men. Even for the experts law is only a prediction of what judges will do under a given set of facts—a prediction that makes rules of law and decisions not logical deductions but functions of human behavior.[2] There are usually plenty of precedents to go around; and with the accumulation of decisions, it is no great problem for the lawyer to find legal authority for most propositions. The difficulty is to estimate what effect a slightly different shade of facts will have and to predict the speed of the current in a changing stream of the law. The predictions and prophecies that lawyers make are indeed appraisals of a host of imponderables. The decisions of yesterday or of the last century are only the starting points.

As for laymen, their conception of the rules of law that govern their conduct is so nebulous that in one sense, as Gray said, the law in its application to their normal affairs is to a very considerable extent *ex post facto*.[3]

The place of *stare decisis* in constitutional law is even more tenuous. A judge looking at a constitutional decision may have compulsions to revere past history and accept what was once written. But he remembers above all else that it is the Constitution which he swore to support and defend, not the gloss which his predecessors may have put on it. So he comes to formulate his own views, rejecting some earlier ones as false and embracing others. He cannot do otherwise unless he lets men long dead and unaware of the problems of the age in which he lives do his thinking for him.

This re-examination of precedent in constitutional law is a personal matter for each judge who comes along. When only one new judge is appointed during a short period, the unsettling effect in constitutional law may not be great. But when a majority of a Court is suddenly reconstituted, there is likely to be substantial unsettlement. There will be unsettlement until the new judges have taken their positions on constitutional doctrine. During that time—which may extend a decade or more—constitutional law will be in flux. That is the necessary consequence of our system and to my mind a healthy one. The alternative is to let the Constitution freeze in the pattern which one generation gave it. But the Constitution was designed for the vicissitudes of time. It must never become a code which carries the overtones of one period that may be hostile to another.

So far as constitutional law is concerned *stare decisis* must give way before the dynamic component of history. Once it does, the cycle starts again. Today's new and startling decision quickly becomes a coveted anchorage for new vested interests. The former proponents of change acquire an acute conservatism in their new *status quo*. It will then take an oncoming group from a new generation to catch the broader vision which may require an undoing of the work of our present and their past.

Much of what courts do is little understood by laymen. Very few portions of the press undertake to show the social, economic, or political significance of the work of the judiciary or to educate the public on long-term trends. Lawyers often do not see the broader view which is exposed by the narrow and intensely personal efforts of a client to vindicate a position or gain an advantage. Yet the work of a court may send a whole economy in one direction or help shape the manifest destiny of an era. Two illustrations from different periods of our history will indicate what I mean.

For at least a decade or more it was commonly assumed that the Fourteenth Amendment was adopted to protect negroes in their newly won rights. Other interests had sought to creep under its wing. Thus corporations claimed they were persons within the meaning of the equal protection clause. Woods (then circuit judge) thought the language of the Amendment and its history too clear to admit of doubt on the point. In 1870 he rejected the contention in *Insurance Co. v. New Orleans*, 1 Woods 85. Sixteen years passed. Woods was now a member of the Court of which Waite was Chief Justice. A railroad company pressed its claim that California's tax assessment against it violated the Equal

Protection Clause of the Fourteenth Amendment. Before the point was even argued, Waite announced from the bench that the Court did not care to hear argument on the question whether the clause applied to corporations. "We are all of opinion that it does," he said.[4] Thus without argument or opinion on the point the *Santa Clara* case became one of the most momentous of all our decisions. It was not long before the same constitutional doctrine was extended to the Due Process Clause.[5] Again the decision was cryptic and oracular, without exposition or explanation.

These decisions, whether right or wrong, sound or unsound, may have changed the course of our industrial history. Corporations were now armed with constitutional prerogatives. And so armed, they proceeded to the development and exploitation of a continent in a manner never equalled before or since. Some think these decisions helped give corporations what Parrington has called "the freedom of buccaneers." [6] They doubtless did release some of the dynamic quality of the drive that built industrial America in a brilliant (albeit ruthless) way.

These unexplained (and certainly not obvious) decisions are now so implicit in the financial and industrial undertaking of the nation that a recent challenge of them had a resounding effect.[7] Such is the hold of *stare decisis* on the profession.

A half century passed and the Court made another decision whose impact on industrial America was almost as profound.

In 1918 the Court in the *Dagenhart* case (*Hammer* v. *Dagenhart*, 247 U. S. 251) had decided that Congress had no power to regulate the production of goods for commerce where the goods themselves were harmless. It thus struck down a child labor law. A process of erosion soon set in. Distinctions and qualifications were made in a long line of decisions. Finally in 1941 in a case involving the constitutionality of the Fair Labor Standards Act (*United States* v. *Darby*, 312 U. S. 100) a unanimous Court overruled the earlier five-to-four decision. Stone's exposition of the Commerce Clause in the *Darby* case was undoubtedly more faithful to Marshall's conception of it[8] than that espoused by a bare majority of the Court in the *Dagenhart* case. However that may be, the *Darby* case gave sanction to a new centralized force in American industrial and social life.

Some have thought that but for the philosophy which it represents and the power of the Federal Government which it sanctions, the nation would not have been able to marshall all the strength and to develop all the ingenuity and resourcefulness necessary to deal with the increasingly national problems of the age.

The decision of the Court in the *Santa Clara* case protected the forces of free enterprise that were building America. We can never know how much the spectre of socialism and the fear of assaults on capitalism contributed to the decision. But the end result is plain: the Court itself became part of the dynamic component of history. It did not live aloof from the turbulence of the times. It was part of the life of the community, absorbed from it the dominant attitudes and feelings of the day, and moved with the impetus of the era.

The Court in the *Darby* case was likewise extremely sensitive to the critical problems of another day. The whole of the democratic world had long been reexamining the conditions that had produced the misery of depressions. It is a soul-searching decision when one is asked to deny the existence of the power of government to correct a social evil. The unanimity of the Court in the *Darby* case indicated how high experience had piled since *Dagenhart* was decided.

Neither the Court in the *Santa Clara* case nor the Court in the *Darby* case was insensitive to the implications of the decisions. Precedents are made or unmade not on logic and history alone. The choices left by the generality of a constitution relate to policy. That is why laymen and lawyers alike must look widely and diversely for understanding. The problem of the judge is to keep personal predilections from dictating the choice and to be as faithful as possible to the architectural scheme. We can get from those who preceded a sense of the continuity of a society. We can draw from their learning a feel for the durability of a doctrine and a sense of the origins of principles. But we have experience that they never knew. Our vision may be shorter or longer. But it is ours. It is better that we make our own history than be governed by the dead. We too must be dynamic components of history if our institutions are to be vital, directive forces in the life of our age.

One can respect the policy decision both in the *Santa Clara* case and in the *Darby* case. But whatever the view on the merits all will agree, I think, that the recent Court was more faithful to the democratic tradition. It wrote in words that all could understand why it did what it did. That is vital to the integrity of the judicial process.

The periods in which the *Santa Clara* and the *Darby* cases were decided were both turbulent. It is of interest to look at them comparatively for insight into the problem of stability of judicial precedents. The latter period closes in some respects a cycle started by the first.

One measure of stability is the extent to which precedents are overruled.

During the thirty-year period between 1860 and 1890, the Court on eighteen occasions overruled (expressly or in effect) controlling precedents. In 10 of these the Court was unanimous. In 13 of the overruled cases the Court had been unanimous. Eight of these cases involved constitutional issues. Ten involved questions of state law and common law and interpretations of statutes.

The most important of the constitutional decisions were the *Legal Tender Cases* (11 Wall. 682, 12 Wall. 457) that overruled the *Hepburn* case (*Hepburn* v. *Griswold*, 8 Wall. 603) decided the previous year. The *Hepburn* case, decided by a 4-3 vote in 1870, held that a creditor need not take United States notes as payment under contracts made prior to the Act of Congress declaring the notes legal tender. The next year the minority of three became a majority of five through the appointment of Strong and Bradley by President Grant.

Feeling of the day ran high. Strange comrades were aligned on both sides of the debate. There was bitter argument by the public. Charges of court-packing reverberated through the country. Many who opposed the first decision likewise opposed the second. The debate shook the country. But the judges then as now spoke their minds. These were men of strong convictions; and they gave the government the flexible control over currency which they thought the Constitution intended.

Hughes once said of this decision, "From the standpoint of the effect on public opinion, there can be no doubt that the reopening of the case was a serious mistake and the overruling in such a short time, and by one vote, of the previous decision shook popular respect for the Court." [9] My own view is different. In some cases it is of course more important that a rule be announced and a dispute put at rest than that a decision be made one way or the other. But when it comes to a constitutional question, especially the authority of government to act, the decision where possible should reflect views of the full court.

The reversal of the Court in the *Legal Tender Cases* had a healthy effect. Management of currency was left in the legislative field, where the school of which Cardozo was a conspicuous member thinks most social and economic problems should remain. It was left so that the people could experiment even unwisely. That is a part of the adventure in democratic government—a view expressed by Bradley in the *Legal Tender Cases*, 12 Wall. p. 562, when he stated, "Questions of political expediency belong to the legislative halls, not to the judicial forum."

In the decade preceding 1860, the Court had held that the admiralty jurisdiction depended on the navigable character of the water, not upon the ebb and flow of the tide thus overruling a leading case from the preceding generation.[10] In the 1868 Term the Court made the foundation of admiralty even firmer by holding, contrary to a ten-year-old decision that admiralty jurisdiction extended to commerce on navigable waters though the transportation was wholly within a state; and further that the action *in rem* was limited to the admiralty court.[11]

In the early part of the period from 1860-1890, the Court gave broad leeway to state regulations of interstate commerce.[12] It sustained a Wisconsin rate even on interstate commerce since Congress had not acted.[13] It held valid a tax on a railroad's gross receipts from interstate commerce.[14] It allowed a State to impose a nondiscriminatory license tax on an interstate business.[15] The first two of these decisions were by a divided Court; the third was unanimous.

But in only a few years important and rather basic shifts on these matters were made. The silence of Congress—the fact that it had not regulated a particular matter—was given increasing weight as evidence of an intent to leave interstate commerce free from regulation. The Court undertook a stricter application of constitutional principles designed to keep the arteries of commerce open and to free the interstate aspects of business from state control whether by taxes or regulation.[16]

State regulation of discriminatory interstate rates of carriers was annulled in the October Term, 1886.[17] In the same Term a unanimous Court held unconstitutional an unapportioned tax on the gross receipts of interstate commerce.[18] The following Term a unanimous Court overturned its previous unanimous decision and held that a license tax on an interstate business was unconstitutional.[19] Shortly thereafter it struck down a state law regulating the sale of liquor in the original package by the importer and with it a forty-three-year-old precedent.[20] Even the evils of alcohol were considered less weighty than the evils of a constrained interstate commerce. Field's view that (apart from strictly local aspects of commerce) the silence of Congress was the "equivalent to its declaration that commerce in the matter shall be free" [21] was in the ascendancy.

In this period the Court also rejected a fifty-nine-year-old precedent and held that Congress had no power to commit for contempt incurred by refusal to obey and respect an order in a Congressional investigation.[22] In the 1824 Term Marshall had ruled that the question whether a suit is against a State within the prohibition of the Eleventh Amendment is determined by reference to the parties of record. After a checkered career that doctrine was finally excised from the law.[23]

These were the eight cases overruling precedents on constitutional law.

The other ten involved more mundane subjects. . . .

A number of decisions in the latter group involved overruling the Court's prior construction of Acts of Congress. These precedents were overruled against objections, at times vigorous, that the correction of the error, if any, should be left to Congress.

In the period from 1937-March 28, 1949, the Court in 30 cases overruled earlier decisions. In 21 of these the reversals were on constitutional grounds. In the great majority of the 30 cases the cases overruled had been decided within the previous 20 years.

These cases are too fresh in memory to require much space for discussion. The largest group—8 in number—related to the taxing power of state and federal governments. Tax rates had become more burdensome than ever before in our history; and tax exemptions were being closely scrutinized as the government's need for revenue grew.

The new approach was largely fashioned by Hughes. He held
for the Court that a nondiscriminatory federal income tax upon
the lessee of a State was not open to the objection that it was a
tax on an instrumentality of the State (*Helvering* v. *Producers
Corp.*, 303 U. S. 376). Two decisions, one from that decade and
one from the preceding decade, fell.[24] The new doctrine was
applied to sustain an Oklahoma estate tax on Indian property[25]
previously held exempt under the federal instrumentality doctrine.[26] And finally in *Oklahoma Tax Commission* v. *Texas Co.*,
decided March 7, 1949, the rest of the cases by which tax immunities had been acquired in Indian property under the instrumentality theory were overruled.[27]

Other private tax exemptions, riding on the concept of sovereign immunity from taxation, were reexamined and eliminated.
Salaries of federal employees were placed within the reach of the
state-taxing power, and the salaries of state employees within the
reach of the national power.[28] A state tax on a private contractor
was upheld, even though its burden would eventually be passed
on to the federal government.[29] This tendency closely to scrutinize tax privileges led to the taxation of the salaries of federal
judges appointed after the taxing statute.[30]

A ten-year-old precedent[31] was overruled and a State was allowed to levy an inheritance tax on shares of a corporation incorporated under its law, although the deceased had been domi-
ciled elsewhere.[32] In another tax case[33] the Court repudiated a
newly spun theory of the privileges and immunity clause[34] which
promised to throttle state power over business affairs.

In other ways too, the Court enlarged the regulatory power of
the States in the field of economic affairs—by a less restrictive
reading of the equal-protection clause;[35] by a more pervasive view
of state regulation of local aspects of interstate industries;[36] by
tolerance of price-fixing by the States.[37]

A judicially created restraint on the power of Congress over
commerce was also removed in the *Darby* case.[38] And contrary
to long-standing rulings on the character of insurance,[39] that
business was held covered by the Sherman Act.[40] During this
period the Court also strengthened the federal eminent domain
power[41] by eliminating private property interests which had
been judicially created in the bed of a navigable stream.[42]

In the field of civil liberties the Court decided and then rather promptly reversed two decisions: it held that a State could not require school children to perform a flag salute in opposition to their religious beliefs[43] and it struck down a license tax imposed on the dissemination of religious literature by a religious group.[44] It also reversed a nine-year-old precedent[45] and held that where a primary election was an integral part of the elective process for nominating candidates for Congress, a State could not exclude a person from the right to vote in it on account of race or color.[46]

In the divorce field the Court reconstrued the Full Faith and Credit Clause so as to give the state of the domicile of one spouse more power over dissolution of the marriage relation.[47]

In *Erie R. Co.* v. *Tompkins*, 304 U. S. 64, the Court rid the federal system of a precedent almost a century old,[48] and with the latter went others that became "obsolete." [49] The Court saw its earlier holding as inviting discrimination by nonresidents of one State against residents of another in diversity cases. It therefore took a step towards uniformity by making local law as construed by state agencies controlling in federal courts in that type of case. And finally in *Lincoln Union* v. *Northwestern Co.*, 335 U. S. 525, decided January 3, 1949, it sustained the constitutionality of state laws outlawing the closed shop. In doing so it repudiated some precedents[50] by which the constitutional standard of Due Process had absorbed economic theories of the judiciary. It returned closer to the earlier constitutional pronouncements that the States have the power "to legislate against what are found to be injurious practices in their internal commercial and business affairs, so long as their laws do not run afoul of some specific federal constitutional prohibition, or of some valid federal law." *Id.*, at p. 536.

Those were the cases reflecting rights-about-face in constitutional law during this recent period. There were others which have been important in the affairs of the nation. A ruling that a utility's depreciation had to be taken at present value rather than cost was rejected.[51] The rule that he who sells an unpatented part of a combination for use in the assembled machine may be guilty of contributory infringement was rejected where a combination patent was being used to protect an unpatented part from competition.[52] It was held that in admiralty the warranty of seaworthiness extended to the appliances and the place of work and that the owner was not relieved of liability because an employee negligently chose defective equipment where sound equipment was available.[53]

In five cases the Court overruled decisions involving interpretations of Acts of Congress and thus cleared the stream of law of derelicts of its own creation, not waiting for Congress to act. It held that private operators of vessels under certain contracts with the government could be sued for torts, the claimants not being restricted to suits against the United States under the Suits in Admiralty Act.[54] It gave a restrictive interpretation to a statute declaratory of the power of federal courts to punish for contempt[55] and thus returned to earlier views of the law. It changed its prior construction of the statute governing naturalization so as to do away with the requirement of an oath to bear arms as a condition of citizenship.[56] It overruled two four-year-old precedents construing the provision of the Revenue Act of 1926 that deals with transfers "intended to take effect in possession or enjoyment" at or after the grantor's death.[57] And just the other day it overruled a nineteen-year-old decision in the same field.[58]

In these cases, as in the ones from the 1860-1890 period already noticed, the Court rejected numerous pleas to let Congress correct mistakes that the Court had created. It was also reluctant to find in the silence of Congress approval of the statutory interpretations which it had adopted.

It is, I think, a healthy practice (too infrequently followed) for a court to re-examine its own doctrine. Legislative correction of judicial errors is often difficult to effect. Moreover, responsible government should entail the undoing of wrongs committed by the department in question. That course is faithful to democratic traditions. Respect for any tribunal is increased if it stands ready (save where injustice to intervening rights would occur)[59] not only to correct the errors of others but also to confess its own. This was the philosophy expressed by a judge of the New York Court of Appeals almost a century ago when he proclaimed it "the duty of every judge and every court to examine its own decisions, . . . without fear, and to revise them without reluctance." [60])That is to heed Shakespeare's warning in *The Merchant of Venice,*

> 'Twill be recorded for a precedent;
> And many an error, by the same example
> Will rush into the state.

I said that one measure of instability in the law is represented by the overruling of precedents. But the overruling itself is at times not the true measure of the change. Commonly the change extended over a long period; the erosion of a precedent was gradual. The overruling did not effect an abrupt change in the law; it rather recognized a *fait accompli*.

In other words the distinguishing of precedents is often a gradual and reluctant way of overruling cases. In modern times the House of Lords has rarely overruled a precedent. But as Radin has shown it has carried the technique of distinguishing precedents "to a very high pitch of ingenuity." [61] And for us the process of distinguishing may indeed do service for overruling or have the same effect, as Brandeis observed in *Burnet* v. *Coronado Oil & Gas Co.*, 285 U. S. 393, 408.

Hammer v. *Dagenhart*, 247 U. S. 251, had a checkered career. Its principle sometimes seemed to be on the wane and then to be restored. It was, for example, held not to forbid federal punishment of the transportation of stolen motor vehicles (*Brooks* v. *United States*, 267 U. S. 432) or of goods made by convict labor (*Kentucky Whip & Collar Co.* v. *Illinois Central R. Co.*, 299 U. S. 334). Yet federal control of the wages, hours and working conditions of miners engaged in producing coal was invalidated (*Carter* v. *Carter Coal Co.*, 298 U. S. 238). But that was the last burst of vitality of the doctrine. *Labor Board* v. *Jones & Laughlin*, 301 U. S. 1, decided in 1937, upheld the Wagner Act as applied to a company producing goods for commerce, and foreshadowed the demise of the *Dagenhart* case. Thus it had been at least substantially impaired before *United States* v. *Darby*, 312 U. S. 100, laid it finally to rest. . . .

Thus the actual overruling of cases is no true measure of the rate of change in the law. The overruling may come at the end of a cycle of change and not mark its commencement. It is this gradual process of erosion of constitutional doctrine that has the true unsettling effect. It is this which often breeds wasteful uncertainty. As the first landmark falls, the outsider may have few clues as to the importance of the shift. The overruling may and often does presage a sweeping change in constitutional doctrine. Years of litigation may be needed to rid the law of mischievous decisions which should have fallen with the first of the series to be overruled.

That is why it is my belief that it would be wise judicial administration when a landmark decision falls to overrule expressly all the cases in the same genus as the one which is repudiated, even though they are not before the Court. There is candor in that course. *Stare decisis* then is not used to breed the uncertainty which it is supposed to dispel.

The development of exceptions or qualifications to constitutional doctrine can have a profound unsettling effect. An excellent example comes from the period 1860-1890.

The power of the states to fix utility rates was a new issue for the Court at that time. The issue was conceived from the conflict between business interests and midwestern farmers, who were rapidly being impoverished by low prices, high interest, and high freight rates. They organized the Grange movement, which succeeded in exerting pressure in midwestern legislatures and obtaining legislation which provided limitations on rates.

It was in this setting that the issue was brought to the Supreme Court in a case involving the power of Illinois to fix the maximum rates for storage of grain in warehouses (*Munn* v. *Illinois*, 94 U. S. 113). A year passed between argument and the rendering of decision in the case. Two important conclusions were reached in this first important case on the subject of rate-making. (1) The power of a State to regulate industries "affected with a public interest" was upheld and the character of business falling in that category was broadly defined. (2) Recourse for correction of the rates was directed to the legislature and not to the courts. Field, in a vigorous dissent, joined in by Strong, viewed the conclusions of the Court as "subversive of the rights of private property" which the judiciary were duty-bound by the Constitution to defend. This dissent backed by the vigor of Field was to have telling effect in succeeding years.

There soon began a process of qualification which narrowed the category of businesses whose prices could be fixed by a State.

The most striking restrictions on legislative power to fix prices were reached in the '20's by a closely divided Court. (*Tyson & Bro.* v. *Banton*, 273 U. S. 418, *Ribnik* v. *McBride*, 277 U. S. 350.) Those decisions marked the floodtide of exceptions and qualifications to the principle of *Munn* v. *Illinois*.

Beginning last century, Field's dissent as to the power of the courts to review utility rates had a powerful influence. There was at first some yielding to Field's view. Then came a change in personnel of the Court. Field's views became the law.[62] In 1890, the Court ruled that the question of reasonableness of rates was not entirely a legislative matter but was ultimately a judicial question arising under the Due Process Clause.[63] Then in 1898, came *Smyth* v. *Ames*, 169 U. S. 466, whose spirit many a judge wished were unblessed. It set constitutional standards for rate-making which haunted utility regulation.

Field's philosophy was that the "present assault upon capital is but the beginning" and only the "stepping-stone to others, larger and more sweeping, till our political contests will become a war of the poor against the rich; a war constantly growing in intensity and bitterness." [64] That philosophy merged with political power to give direction to the age. The spectre of confiscation rode high. Security was thought to be dependent upon keeping capital unfettered.

Today there is greater realization that survival lies in the development of a cooperative society where the security of capital rests on the broad base of the prosperity of the multitude. Today the accepted view is that property need not be made tyrant in order to give men freedom and incentive to acquire it, own it, and manage it and to unleash the great productive power of free enterprise.

Much of the unsettling influence of the Court since 1937 has been in removing from constitutional doctrine excrescences produced early in the century. The tendency has been to return to older views of constitutional interpretation, and to sanction governmental power over social and economic affairs which the Court beginning in the '80's and particularly in the preceding ten to thirty years had denied. Only if this is understood can the work of the period be put into clear historical perspective.

As respects price-fixing the process of restoration of the principle of *Munn* v. *Illinois* started almost at once after the flood of exceptions and qualifications had been reached. The ebb was clear and distinct.[65] The tide had started running back to *Munn* v. *Illinois* at least by 1934 when *Nebbia* v. *New York*, 291 U. S. 502, upheld the power of New York to fix the retail price of milk. *Olsen* v. *Nebraska*, 313 U. S. 236, decided April 28, 1941, merely marked the low tide. We returned in less than 70 years substantially to our starting point. *Munn* v. *Illinois* regained its lost vitality so far as price-fixing was concerned. Field's fear that "the prices of everything, from a calico gown to a city mansion, may be the subject of legislative direction" (94 U. S. p. 152) came true.

But that was only one phase of a basic shift in constitutional doctrine which took place during the recent period. Waite in *Munn* v. *Illinois* expressed in homely and unsophisticated terms the importance of judicial self-denial in review of social legislation. It was the view so ably espoused in later years by Holmes, Brandeis, Cardozo, and Stone. In *Munn* v. *Illinois*, 94 U. S. p. 134, Waite said, "For protection against abuses by legislatures the people must resort to the polls, not to the courts."

That principle was largely abandoned in the intervening years. The courts became the place to get relief from the pinch of legislation deemed to be improvident and unwise or hostile to the dominant interests of the day. But in the period from 1937-1949 Waite's view has been in process of restoration. The wisdom of legislation is to be tested by political processes, not by litigation. There are numerous instances during the recent period where that view has been applied. The recent closed-shop decision (*Lincoln Union* v. *Northwestern Co.*, 335 U. S. 525) is perhaps the best example. In the whole field of social legislation we have in a sense closed the cycle by returning to the philosophy of *Munn* v. *Illinois* and by wiping out the large group of intervening decisions which were hostile to legislative power and jealous of judicial power.[66]

The weakening of Field's influence on judicial review of utility rates has not been as complete. The force of the precedents forged in his era (and later strengthened by *Smyth* v. *Ames*, 169 U. S. 466) has been considerably dissipated, though they have not been overruled. Recent cases,[67] however, adopted a more pragmatic basis for rate-making, though the full-blown rule of legislative power in rate-making which *Munn* v. *Illinois* sponsored was not restored.

There are other factors of change and unsettlement in the law which defy statistical treatment. A rule of law correcting a social evil may be announced. But if it is not applied in the life of the community, there is no change. In spite of a new and unsettling pronouncement the course of the law may go on its way, undisturbed. On the other hand, if the Court as a matter of judicial administration pursues the matter and applies the principle with care and vigor in case after case, the effect of the change may be profound. We can only tell whether the Court is working in that direction by examining the cases which it takes and the manner of its disposition of them.

On what manner of cases does the Court spend its time? How is the discretionary certiorari jurisdiction employed? To what problems is the Court giving emphasis?

A few examples from the current period will illustrate how this matter of emphasis has caused substantial changes in law administration and in statutory interpretation.

There has been increasing scrutiny of charges that confessions in criminal cases were coerced and a growing hostility to traces of third-degree methods of the police in criminal prosecutions.[68] There has been an increasing attention to the constitutional requirement of counsel in criminal cases.[69] One product of that scrutiny has been fundamental changes in the practice in some States, notably Missouri and Illinois.[70] There has been increasing attention to Federal Employer Liability Act cases that an indifferent or unfriendly attitude had permeated with a philosophy hostile to that reflected in the legislation.[71]

The study of changes in judicial precedents gives, of course, a distorted view. It is like the study of pathological cases in social or medical sciences. The norm is robust and enduring. The case that gets into the books often has an unsettling effect. Yet we are apt to forget that "the fact that a case is in the reports at all is in itself uncertain." [72] The great body of law is unperturbed by events that may rock a nation.

When the changing stream of public law is studied there are three considerations to keep in mind.

First. We have had only one major dispute that struck at the vitals of our federalism. That was the Civil War. Our controversies and quarrels even at the level of constitutional law have been of a lesser kind. They have been disputes calling for adjustment within the framework of our Charter not for repudiation of it. As one of my Brethren recently stated,[73] they have not involved reconsideration of our basic constitutional tenets which have been accepted since the days of Marshall. They have entailed argument over the application of established doctrine. The problem has been to free the system for growth unhampered by the crippling restraints which men of cramped and narrow vision placed on it. In considering the charges leveled against those of any period who are responsible for giving new or broader interpretations to the Constitution or discarding precedents it is well to remember these words of Thayer,[74]

And so it happens, as one looks back over our history and the field of political discussions in the past, that he seems to see the whole region strewn with the wrecks of the Constitution—of what people have been imagining and putting forward as the Constitution. That it was unconstitutional to buy Louisiana and Florida; that it was unconstitutional to add new states to the Union from territory not belonging originally to it; that it was unconstitutional to govern the territories at all; that it was unconstitutional to charter a bank, to issue paper money, to make it a legal tender, to enact a protective tariff,—that these and a hundred other things were a violation of the Constitution has been solemnly and passionately asserted by statesmen and lawyers. Nothing that is now going forward can exceed the vehemence of denunciation, and the pathetic and conscientious resistance of those who lifted up their voices against many of these supposed violations of the Constitution. The trouble has been, then as now, that men imputed to our fundamental law their own too narrow construction of it, their own theory of its purposes and its spirit, and sought thus, when the question was one of mere power, to restrict its great liberty.

Second. It is sometimes thought to be astute political management of a shift in position to proclaim that no change is under way. That is designed as a sedative to instill confidence and allay doubts. It has been a tool of judges as well as other officials.

Precedents, though distinguished and qualified out of existence, apparently have been kept alive. The theory is that the outward appearance of stability is what is important.

The idea that any body of law, particularly public law, should appear to stay put and not be in flux is an interesting phenomenon that Frank has explored in *Law and Modern Mind*. He points out how it is—in law and in other fields too—that men continue to chant of the immutability of a rule in order to "cover up the transformation, to deny the reality of change, to conceal the truth of adaptation behind a verbal disguise of fixity and universality." [75] But the more blunt, open, and direct course is truer to democratic traditions. It reflects the candor of Cardozo. The principle of full disclosure has as much place in government as it does in the market place. A judiciary that discloses what it is doing and why it does it will breed understanding. And confidence based on understanding is more enduring than confidence based on awe.

Third. From age to age the problem of constitutional adjudication is the same. It is to keep the power of government unrestrained by the social or economic theories that one set of judges may entertain. It is to keep one age unfettered by the fears or limited vision of another. There is in that connection one tenet of faith which has crystallized more and more as a result of our long experience as a nation. It is this: If the social and economic problems of state and nation can be kept under political management of the people, there is likely to be long-run stability. It is when a judiciary with life tenure seeks to write its social and economic creed into the Charter that instability is created. For then the nation lacks the adaptability to master the sudden storms of an era. It must be remembered that the process of constitutional amendment is a long and slow one.

That philosophy is reflected in what Thomas Jefferson wrote about the Constitution.[76]

Some men look at constitutions with sanctimonious reverence, and deem them like the ark of the covenant, too sacred to be touched. They ascribe to the men of the preceding age a wisdom more than human, and suppose what they did to be beyond amendment. I knew that age well; I belonged to it, and labored with it. It deserved well of its country. It was very like the present, but without the experience of the present; and forty years of experience in govern-ment is worth a century of book-reading; and this they would say themselves, were they to rise from the dead.

Jefferson's words are *a fortiori* germane to the fashioning of constitutional law and to the lesser lawmaking in which the ju-diciary necessarily indulges.

REFERENCES

[1] See *United States* v. *Title Ins. Co.*, 265 U. S. 472, 486-487.

[2] Holmes, The Path of the Law, 10 Harv. L. Rev. 457, 459-461; Cohen, Transcendental Nonsense and The Functional Approach, 35 Col. L. Rev. 809, 842 *et seq.*; Moore, Rational Basis of Legal Institutions, 23 Col. L. Rev. 609; Frank, Law and the Modern Mind, pp. 100-159.

[3] Gray, The Nature and Sources of Law, § 225.

[4] *Santa Clara Co.* v. *Southern Pac. R. Co.*, 118 U. S. 394, 396.

[5] *Minneapolis R. Co.* v. *Beckwith*, 129 U. S. 26, 28, decided in 1889.

[6] Main Currents in American Thought.

[7] Black dissenting in *Connecticut General Co.* v. *Johnson*, 303 U. S. 77, 85.

[8] *Gibbons* v. *Ogden*, 9 Wheat. 1, 196.

[9] Hughes, The Supreme Court of the United States, p. 52.

[10] *The Thomas Jefferson*, 10 Wheat. 428 overruling *The Genesee Chief*, 12 How. 443.

[11] *The Belfast*, 7 Wall. 624, overruling *Allen* v. *Newbury*, 21 How. 244.

[12] These decisions, like *Munn* v. *Illinois*, 94 U. S. 135, itself, reflected the tolerance for local regulations expressed in *Cooley* v. *Board of Wardens*, 12 How. 299, 319.

[13] *Peik* v. *Chicago & N. Ry. Co.*, 94 U. S. 164.

[14] *State Tax on Railway Gross Receipts*, 15 Wall. 284.

[15] *Osborne* v. *Mobile*, 16 Wall. 479.

[16] For longer and more fundamental cyclical swings under the Commerce Clause see Rutledge, A Declaration of Legal Faith; Ribble, State and National Power over Commerce.

[17] *Wabash, St. L. & P. Ry. Co.* v. *Illinois*, 118 U. S. 557.

[18] *Philadelphia Steamship Co.* v. *Pennsylvania*, 122 U. S. 326.

[19] *Leloup* v. *Port of Mobile*, 127 U. S. 640.

[20] *Leisy* v. *Hardin*, 135 U. S. 100, overruling *Pierce* v. *New Hampshire*, 5 How. 504.

[21] *Bowman* v. *Chicago & N. Ry. Co.*, 125 U. S. 465, 508.

[22] *Kilbourn* v. *Thompson*, 103 U. S. 168, overruling *Anderson* v. *Dunn*, 6 Wheat. 204.

[23] *In re Ayres*, 123 U. S. 443, overruling in part *Osborn* v. *U. S. Bank*, 9 Wheat. 738.

[24] *Gillespie* v. *Oklahoma*, 257 U. S. 501; *Burnet* v. *Coronado Oil & Gas Co.*, 285 U. S. 393.

[25] *Oklahoma Tax Comm'n* v. *United States*, 319 U. S. 598.

[26] *Childers* v. *Beaver*, 270 U. S. 555.

[27] *Howard* v. *Gipsy Oil Co.*, 247 U. S. 503; *Large Oil Co.* v. *Howard*, 248 U. S. 549; *Oklahoma* v. *Barnsdall Refineries*, 296 U. S. 521; *Choctaw & Gulf R. Co.* v. *Harrison*, 235 U. S. 292; *Indian Oil Co.* v. *Oklahoma*, 240 U. S. 522.

[28] Graves v. New York ex rel. O'Keefe, 306 U. S. 466, overruling *Collector v. Day*, 11 Wall. 113 and New York ex rel. Rogers v. Graves, 299 U. S. 401.

[29] Alabama v. *King & Boozer*, 314 U. S. 1, overruling *Panhandle Oil Co. v. Knox*, 277 U. S. 218 and Graves v. Texas Co., 298 U. S. 393.

[30] O'Malley v. Woodrough, 307 U. S. 277, overruling *Miles v. Graham*, 268 U. S. 501.

[31] First National Bank v. Maine, 284 U. S. 312.

[32] State Tax Commission v. Aldrich, 316 U. S. 174.

[33] Madden v. Kentucky, 309 U. S. 83.

[34] Colgate v. Harvey, 296 U. S. 404.

[35] Tigner v. Texas, 310 U. S. 141, overruling *Connolly v. Union Sewer Pipe Co.*, 184 U. S. 540.

[36] California v. Thompson, 313 U. S. 109, overruling *Di Santo v. Pennsylvania*, 273 U. S. 34.

[37] Olsen v. Nebraska, 313 U. S. 236, overruling *Ribnik v. McBride*, 277 U. S. 350.

[38] United States v. Darby, 312 U. S. 100, reversing *Hammer v. Dagenhart*, 247 U. S. 251.

[39] Paul v. Virginia, 8 Wall. 168.

[40] United States v. Underwriters Ass'n., 322 U. S. 533.

[41] United States v. Chicago, M. St. P. & P. R. Co., 312 U. S. 592.,

[42] United States v. Lynah, 188 U. S. 445.

[43] Board of Education v. Barnette, 319 U. S. 624, overruling *Minersville School Dist. v. Gobitis*, 310 U. S. 586.

[44] Jones v. Opelika, 319 U. S. 103, overruling *Jones v. Opelika*, 316 U. S. 584.

[45] Grovey v. Townsend, 295 U. S. 45.

[46] Smith v. Allwright, 321 U. S. 649.

[47] Williams v. North Carolina, 317 U. S. 287, overruling *Haddock v. Haddock*, 201 U. S. 562, and Sherrer v. Sherrer, 334 U. S. 343, overruling in part, *Andrews v. Andrews*, 188 U. S. 14.

[48] Swift v. Tyson, 16 Pet. 1.

[49] Cf. Angel v. Bullington, 330 U. S. 183, 194, with *Lupton's Sons Co. v. Automobile Club*, 225 U. S. 489.

[50] Adair v. United States, 208 U. S. 161, and Coppage v. Kansas, 236 U. S. 1.

[51] Federal Power Commission v. Hope Gase Co., 320 U. S. 591, overruling that part of *United Railways v. West*, 280 U. S. 234.

[52] Mercoid Corp. v. Mid-Continent Co., 320 U. S. 661, overruling *Leeds & Catlin Co. v. Victor Talking Machine Co.* (No. 2), 213 U. S. 325.

[53] Mahnich v. Southern S. S. Co., 321 U. S. 96, overruling *Plamals v. Pinar Del Rio*, 277 U. S. 151.

[54] Brady v. Roosevelt S.S. Co., 317 U. S. 575, overruling *Fleet Corp. v. Lustgarten*, 280 U. S. 320.

[55] Nye v. United States, 313 U. S. 33, overruling *Toledo Newspaper Co. v. United States*, 247 U. S. 402.

[56] Girouard v. United States, 328 U. S. 61, overruling *United States v. Schwimmer*, 279 U. S. 644, United States v. Macintosh, 283 U. S. 605, United States v. Bland, 283 U. S. 636.

[57] Helvering v. Hallock, 309 U. S. 106, overruling *Helvering v. St. Louis Trust Co.*, 296 U. S. 39, and Becker v. St. Louis Trust Co., 296 U. S. 48.

[58] Commissioner v. Church, 335 U. S. 632, overruling *May v. Heiner*, 281 U. S. 238.

[59] On the prospective overruling of precedents to prevent such hardship see *Great Northern Ry. Co. v. Sunburst Co.*, 287 U. S. 358; Aero Spark Plug Co. v. B. G. Corporation, 130 F. 2d 290, 296-299.

[60] Baker v. Lorillard, 4 N. Y. 257, 261.

[61] The Trail of the Calf, 32 Corn. L.Q. 137, 143.

[62] See *Federal Power Commission v. Natural Gas Pipeline Co.*, 315 U. S. 575, 600.

[63] *Chicago, M. & St. P. R. Co. v. Minnesota*, 134 U. S. 418.

[64] See *Pollock v. Farmers Loan & Trust Co.*, 157 U. S. 429, 607.

[65] See *Tagg Bros. v. United States*, 280 U. S. 420; *O'Gorman & Young v. Hartford Fire Ins. Co.*, 282 U. S. 251.

[66] The durability of *Munn v. Illinois* on another point should be mentioned. Waite ruled that grain warehouses though instruments of interstate commerce could be regulated by the States until Congress acted (94 U. S. p. 135). Congress did act in 1916. By the United States Warehouse Act (39 Stat. 486) it made federal regulation subservient to state regulation. In 1931 it altered the scheme of the Act, making federal regulation exclusive of state regulation as respects the matters covered by the federal act. See *Rice v. Santa Fe Elevator Corp.*, 331 U. S. 218.

[67] *Federal Power Commission v. Natural Gas Pipeline Co.*, 315 U. S. 575; *Federal Power Commission v. Hope Gas Co.*, 320 U. S. 591.

[68] See *Chambers v. Florida*, 309 U. S. 227; *Ashcraft v. Tennessee*, 322 U. S. 143; *Malinski v. New York*, 324 U. S. 401; *Haley v. Ohio*, 332 U. S. 596.

[69] See *Williams v. Kaiser*, 323 U. S. 471; *Hawk v. Olson*, 326 U. S. 271; *De Meerleer v. Michigan*, 329 U. S. 663.

[70] Rule 27A, 400 Ill. 22; Judicial Conference of Missouri, Executive Council, Special Report No. 3, February 8, 1945; Special Report No. 4, February 20, 1945. Special Report No. 9, November 8, 1945. See also 1 Journ. of Missouri Bar 73; 2 Journ. of Missouri Bar. 17, 28.

[71] See *Wilkerson v. McCarthy*, 335 U. S. —, for a review of these cases since the 1943 Term.

[72] Radin, The Trail of the Calf, 32 Corn. L.Q. 137, 148.

[73] Reed, Stare Decisis and Constitutional Law, 35 Penna. Bar Assoc. Quart. 131, 139-140. "No responsible official, jurist or statesman, has ever suggested that an effort should be made to ask reconsideration of the doctrine of dual sovereignty, the separation of powers or the supremacy of the Federal Constitution. It is the applications of the established doctrine that fill the courts and, indeed, the nation with controversy. Those applications are properly and continuously subject to critical reexamination. No threat of a challenge to established constitutional principles is on the horizon. The most likely controversies as to constitutional principle, in the immediate future, will be over the interrelation or interaction of one principle upon another."

[74] Legal Essays, p. 158.

[75] Law and The Modern Mind, p. 293. Cf. Fortas & Chisholm, The Psychiatry of Enduring Peace and Social Progress, 9 Journ. Biol. & Path. of Interpersonal Rel. 1, 3.

[76] Letter to Samuel Kercheval, July 12, 1816.

WILLIAM J. BRENNAN, JR.

ASSOCIATE JUSTICE, 1956—

Law and Social Sciences[*]

It has been suggested that perhaps law—in the sense that I shall use the word, namely, law making and law declaring—is the only true social science and that the other disciplines which claim to that category are usurpers of the title. This pretension proceeds from the premise that law in action determines which adjustments of human relationships are in fact compatible with the realization of democratic ideals—that it is the lawyer's mastery over constitutions, statutes, appellate opinions and textbooks of peculiar idiom, and his skill in operating the mechanics of governmental institutions, courts, legislatures, administrative boards, executive offices, and private associations, corporations, partnerships, trade associations, labor unions—that set him apart from, and give him a certain advantage over diplomats, economists, social psychologists, social historians, biologists and the other skilled groups.

I do not propose to take sides in that debate. My purpose is to develop the conclusion, I hope persuasively, that in the onrushing atomic age, the realization and preservation of democratic ideals demand that the legal profession, on which society has laid the primary responsibility to be the protector of those ideals—to take the lead in realizing them—must not grudgingly, but rather designedly and thoroughly, avail itself of the wisdom other disciplines provide, lest democratic values be lost.

Necessarily we must first agree on what democratic values are, and why it is the practitioners of the law have a special role in their attainment and preservation.

[*] From the Gaston Lecture, Georgetown University, Washington, D. C. Printed in 24 Vital Speeches 143 (1957). Reprinted by permission of Mr. Justice Brennan and the publisher. Footnotes omitted.

The democratic ideal has been variously stated. Professors Lasswell and McDougal have epitomized it, I think, as well as any. Say they: "The supreme value of democracy is the dignity and worth of the individual; hence a democratic society is a commonwealth of mutual deference—a commonwealth where there is full opportunity to mature talent into socially creative skill, free from discrimination on grounds of religion, culture, or class. It is a society in which such specific values as power, respect and knowledge are widely shared and are not concentrated in the hands of a single group, class or institution—the state—among the many institutions of society." The great importance of the lawyer's role in the common task of achieving this most difficult of all ways of life derives from the very practical fact that the lawyer is the roving fullback of our society with his nose stuck into every activity in which we severally participate. This has been a marked development of the last half century, and necessarily so as the rule of law has loomed larger and larger as the essential stabilizer of the complex organism society has become. . . .

More than ever is the lawyer the policy maker whether in legislative halls, where he has complete dominance; on the bench, which is his monopoly; as practitioner, where his advice is indispensable to men of every calling; or in commerce, industry, and other pursuits where increasingly he occupies seats of power.

Arthur T. Vanderbilt has noted that "it can no longer be maintained that the law can be isolated from the other social sciences or understood without them. Holmes anticipated all of this when he said: 'It is perfectly proper to regard and study the law simply as a great anthropological document.' And again: 'If your subject is law, the roads are plain to anthropology, the science of man, to political economy, the theory of legislation, ethics, and thus by several paths to your final view of life.' It was Holmes, too, who prophesied half a century ago: 'For the rational study of the law the black letter man may be the man of the present, but the man of the future is the man of statistics and the master of economics.'

"As industry and society have become more complex and as the social aspects of the law have necessarily increased, the interrelation of law and the social sciences has become more and more manifest and the sociological school of jurisprudence, of which Dean Pound is the exponent, has had great influence on the trend of legal thinking. It was Louis D. Brandeis, the lawyer, however, who was the pioneer in the use of social facts in litigation, insisting that 'Out of the facts grows the law,' a theme that was to find later utterance in his judicial opinions, and that will doubtless increasingly influence the course of our judicial decisions in the future." Enormous social changes are bound to follow the stupendous scientific advances of the age at the threshold of which we now stand, uncertain and perhaps not a little afraid. It is a time when, as Judge Wyzanski has observed, "men have come to wonder whether the older values are fully adequate and whether there has not been a degree of deception with respect to the absolutism previously claimed for the older values." Can the developing law, rightly viewed as continuously more effective social engineering, any longer isolate itself from the other disciplines, each of themselves also achieving greater perfection in the study of the human condition pertinent to its role in mirroring our complex social organism.

We cannot deny that the positivistic tradition in law is a hardy growth in America, and not without reason.

A society obviously plural in its pursuit of ultimate ends has good reason to fear the monopolization of the coercive power of the state in the pursuit of objectives not necessarily agreeable to all. The enactment of today's moral law, qua morality rather than for any peculiarly social objectives, is frightening precisely because of what may be enacted in the name of morality tomorrow, by others who have captured the legislative or judicial processes. Moreover, so many values arising from or demanded by the human condition are valuable precisely because they are the product of or obtained by the uncoerced human will and mind. Positive law, although it can create a climate favorable to their growth, if it coercively attempts by the sanctions available to it to create these values, destroys them in the process. St. Paul speaks of the new dispensation as beyond "the law." Although he did not mean law in the narrow sense of human enactment that we are now dealing with, his words stand as a permanent warning and reminder of that vast range of ends that lies beyond the rule-making power of court or legislature.

Drawing on the tradition generated by these considerations, legal thinkers in England and America, and to a lesser extent on the continent where the influence of Roman law and Natural Law was most strongly felt, attempted during the Nineteenth Century to meet the demands of these fears by progressively isolating law from other disciplines, particularly from theology and from philosophy that was not expressly legal philosophy. They thought thereby to avoid the danger that the instrumentality of law would be captured for the use of particular ends which were not properly the ends of society as a whole. Of course, they ran the risk that law might in this manner be rendered useless for the pursuit of any ends whatsoever, even the proper ends of society. We think, of course, of Austin and his attempt to "purify" law by the reduction to the formula of the sovereign will. Closer to home, we think of the constant insistence of some on law as the science of observation and prediction, prediction as to what the law maker is likely to do. They are concerned in Holmes' phrase with the "cutting edge" of the law; in seeing where and in what pattern the sanctions of the law are applied. This is "*the* law" and from the observer's point of view it is a law wholly unconcerned with the broader, extra legal values pursued by society at large or the individual.

It must be obvious that this approach is of little assistance to one concerned with the creation of law. It serves him ill to be concerned with predicting his own actions. It provides no guide to what action to take and what laws to enact. His is the hard task of making law. And who is this man? I repeat, in the first instance he is today the legislator, so styled. But it is obvious to all of us who in any way have touched the law and passed beyond the naive conception of the layman who thinks it is all in the statutes, that he is also the judge, the practicing lawyer, and the legal scholar. As Mr. Justice Traynor of the California Supreme Court has said: "More than ever social problems find their solution in legislation. Endless problems remain, however, which the courts must resolve without benefit of legislation. The great mass of cases are decided within the confines of stare decisis. Yet there is a steady evolution, for it is not quite true that there is nothing new under the sun; rarely is a case identical with the ones that went before. Courts have a creative job to do when they find that a rule has lost its touch with reality and should be abandoned or reformulated to meet new conditions and new moral values. And in those cases where there is no stare decisis to cast its light or shadow, the courts must hammer out new rules that will respect whatever values of the past have survived the tests of reason and experience and anticipate what contemporary values will best meet those tests. The task is not easy—human relations are infinitely complex, and subtlety and depth of spirit must enter into their regulation. Often legal problems elude any final solution, and courts then can do no more than find what Cardozo called the least erroneous answers to insoluble problems. But a searching error is a useful worm, burrowing deep to leaven the hard ground of tradition that it may nourish new growth as dogma dies."

So it is that on the same facts judges will often differ in their conclusions. "It is in the area between established fact and the pertinent principles of the law that the law itself grows. It is here that the changing mores of a people come into play in bringing the law into agreement with the advancing insights and the emerging needs of society. Thus experience in the analysis of human problems once more supports the argument that the humanistic disciplines should play a large part in general education of the future lawyer." . . .

The legal scholar's role is, par excellence, a creative one. He is more likely to have the leisure and range of thought necessary to reach across the arbitrary divisions between disciplines in the academic world and sense values that the law may properly serve and techniques it may profitably use. It is not chance that a news columnist recently attacked law reviews and what he considered their improper influence on judicial decisions. The mind of the layman unfamiliar with the judicial process supposes it to exist in the air, as a self-justifying and wholly independent process. The opposite is of course true, that judicial decision must be nourished by all the insights that scholarship can furnish and legal scholarship must in turn be nourished by all the disciplines that comprehend the totality of human experience.

The tradition that I shall call "the isolationist tradition" in the law is of relatively recent origin in the West. In an earlier age, it would have been thought folly that law should serve only its own symmetry rather than ends defined by other disciplines. It is not chance that the word law has in the European tradition embraced so many different concepts. The phrase Natural Law, for example, had with the Romans, the schoolmen of the Middle

Ages, and the philosophers of the Enlightenment, wholly different meanings. This rich confusion of meanings points to a continuing realization, which we must ever encourage, especially in our law schools, that the discipline of the law, as we are now narrowly speaking of it, cannot live of itself.

Casual reflection furnishes numerous examples of periods in which law was merged, perhaps now we would say, too thoroughly merged, with the other disciplines and sources of human value. Custom, for example, was always the common law's most cherished source. So much so, in fact, that not until well into the Seventeenth Century did English lawyers make any clear distinction between law declaring and law making. And what was declared custom but the accumulated wisdom on social problems of society itself? The function of law was to formalize and preserve this wisdom, but it certainly did not purport to originate it. St. Thomas, as you all know, in complete agreement with the Greek tradition both in its Aristotelian and Platonic modes was forever concerned with seeing things whole. His treatise on positive, human law does not stand alone, but is part of a general analysis of the whole human situation, and draws its validity from its position in the entire scheme of things. Anyone who wants a particularly vivid example of the fusion between law and the ultimate ends of man and society, has only to read the decrees of Charlemagne. He thought it preeminently appropriate to put his rule-making authority to the realization of the Christian ideal and the salvation of the souls of his subjects in a most thoroughgoing manner. Ecclesiastical and monastic reform, for example, were achieved, and quite properly it was thought, by imperial decree. I hasten to add that I cherish no such program for the United States but cite these examples to stimulate our thinking and fructify our imagination on this subject. The isolationist theory of law is not the only one, nor, do I think it is one that this country by the shape of its institutions must necessarily cherish. On the contrary, the job at hand is to create a realization, particularly among our law students, that the law is not an end in itself, nor does it provide ends. It is preeminently a means to serve what we think is right. Government, it has been said, is a menial task. I think we can accept the truth of the statement, without accepting the disparaging connotations. Law is here to serve! To serve what? To serve, insofar as law can properly do so, within limits that I have already stressed, the realization of man's ends, ultimate and mediate.

In this task lawyers must turn their minds to the knowledge and experience of the other disciplines, and in particular to those disciplines that investigate and report on the functioning and nature of society. The lawyer is accustomed to the use of history in this regard, because the common law particularly is the creature of history and growth. But the lawyer is much less used to valuing and examining the other, less firmly established sociological disciplines. I know that there are still some who so firmly believe that the law should not consult the wisdom of the other disciplines as to meet this proposal with scorn and demand that the profession keep to its own business, whatever that is. Surely the lawyer's business is broader than these critics suppose, and the profession would shirk its responsibility if it neglected any source of wisdom that could reasonably be thought to assist the better doing of the profession's really difficult task. . . .

President Kiewiet of the University of Rochester said what I am attempting to convey. "The life of every society contains an unending contest between the forces of stability and change. To change too little may lead to stagnation and death; to change too much may lead to disaster and collapse. Yet the thrust of revolution is upon our generation. Some of the thrust must be resisted if we are to live according to the lights history has given us. Yet we must know that even then we shall have to accept and make possible great changes in our society. The law is utterly caught up in the immense crisis of our generation. Upon those who practice the law rests a great share of the delicate responsibility of deciding what must be preserved and what must be changed, what we shall protect and what we shall abandon."

PART FOUR

Liberty and Judicial Review

"[A] cult of libertarian judicial activists now assails the Court almost as bitterly for renouncing power as the earlier 'liberals' once did for assuming too much power. This cult appears to believe that the Court can find in a 4,000-word eighteenth-century document or its nineteenth-century Amendments, or can plausibly supply, some clear bulwark against all dangers and evils that beset us internally. This assumes that the Court will be the dominant factor in shaping the constitutional practice of the future and can and will maintain, not only equality with the elective branches, but a large measure of supremacy and control over them. I may be biased against this attitude because it is so contrary to the doctrines of the critics of the Court, of whom I was one, at the time of the Roosevelt proposal to reorganize the judiciary. But it seems to me a doctrine wholly incompatible with faith in democracy, and in so far as it encourages a belief that judges may be left to correct the result of public indifference to issues of liberty in choosing Presidents, Senators, and Representatives, it is a vicious teaching."

Mr. Justice Jackson

"Some people regard the prohibitions of the Constitution, even its most unequivocal commands, as mere admonitions which Congress need not always observe. . . . I cannot accept this approach to the Bill of Rights. It is my belief that there *are* 'absolutes'. . . . [There is] no justification whatever for 'balancing' a particular right against some expressly granted power of Congress. If the Constitution withdraws from government all power over subject matter in an area, such as religion, speech, press, assembly, and petition, there is nothing over which authority may be exerted. . . . The great danger of the judiciary balancing process is that in times of emergency and stress it gives Government the power to do what it thinks necessary to protect itself, regardless of the rights of individuals. . . . In effect, it changes the direction of our form of government from a government of limited powers to a government in which Congress may do anything that Courts believe to be 'reasonable'."

Mr. Justice Black

ROBERT H. JACKSON

ASSOCIATE JUSTICE, 1941-1954

The Supreme Court as a Political Institution[*]

Few accusations against the Supreme Court are made with more heat and answered with less candor than that it makes political decisions. Of course, the line between political science and legal science is not fixed and varies with one's definition of his terms. Any decision that declares the law under which a people must live or which affects the powers of their institutions is in a very real sense political. I have previously quoted Judge Cardozo, who contrasted the New York Court of Appeals and the United States Supreme Court in these terms: "It [the New York Court of Appeals] is a great common law court; its problems are lawyers' problems. But the Supreme Court is occupied chiefly with statutory construction—which no man can make interesting—and with politics." [1] Of course, he used "politics" in no sense of partisanship but in the sense of policy-making. His remarks point to some features of the federal judicial power which distinguish it from the functions of the usual law court.

As already noted, the Constitutional Convention deliberately withheld from the Supreme Court power that was political in form, such as a forthright power to veto or revise legislation, and in that spirit the Court has held itself without power to render advisory opinions for the guidance even of the President.

The Court has also observed a number of other self-limitations which are intended to keep it out of active participation in the political processes. It has refused to inquire whether a state gov-

[*] Reprinted by permission of the publishers from Robert H. Jackson, *The Supreme Court in the American System of Government.* Cambridge, Mass., Harvard University Press, pp. 52-83. Copyright, 1955, by William Eldred Jackson and G. Gowdoin Craighill, Jr., Executors. Footnotes renumbered.

ernment complies with the guarantee of a republican form of government[2] or has properly ratified a proposed constitutional amendment.[3] It has given finality to the certification by the other branches of government that a federal statute is as signed, as against a claim of variance with the language actually adopted.[4] The duration of a state of war,[5] the abrogation of treaties,[6] the recognition or nonrecognition of foreign governments,[7] and matters of foreign policy[8] generally, have been held to be political questions.

Even more controversial has been the effort to use the Supreme Court to control the districting of states for the elections of members of Congress,[9] to fix the terms on which a new political party may go on the state ballot,[10] and to abolish the "county unit" system used in some states.[11] Of course, it would be nice if there were some authority to make everybody do the things we ought to have done and leave undone the things we ought not to have done. But are the courts the appropriate catch-all into which every such problem should be tossed? One can answer "Yes" if some immediate political purpose overshadows concern for the judicial institution. But in most such cases interference by the Court would take it into matters in which it lacks special competence, let alone machinery of implementation.

The judicial power of the Supreme Court, however, does extend to all cases arising under the Constitution, to controversies to which the United States is a party, and to those between two or more states. Thus, the Court must face political questions in legal form, for surely a controversy between two separately organized political societies does present a political question, even if waged with the formalities of a lawsuit. And any decision which confirms, allocates, or shifts power as between different branches of the Federal Government or between it and a constituent state is equally political, no matter whether the decision be reached by a legislative or a judicial process. Our Constitution was the product and expression of a virile political philosophy held by those who wrote it. Controversies over its meaning often spring from political motives, for the object of politics always is to obtain power. Such controversies have to be solved either by consideration of the experiences and statements of the framers which indicate the original will, or by reference to some relevant subsequent events and currents of opinion deemed controlling. And all constitutional interpretations have political consequences.

We must not forget that, at bottom, the Civil War was fought over constitutional doctrine. It oversimplifies that tragedy to say that it was a war over slavery, an institution which many southern leaders had come to deplore and one which Mr. Lincoln did not propose to abolish in the states where it existed. The controversy was over the power of the Federal Government to control the spread of slavery into new territory, and over the voluntary or compulsory character of the federal compact. These, like most other questions which have deeply agitated our people, found their way to the Supreme Court in the guise of private controversies between litigating parties.

Only those heedless of legal history can deny that in construing the Constitution the Supreme Court from time to time makes new constitutional law or alters the law that has been. And it is idle to say that this is merely the ordinary process of interpretation, as in the law of negotiable instruments, for example. While a vast and respectable body of learning on the law of bills and notes existed in the Western World, the federal judiciary was not bound to apply it. The Supreme Court had even less jurisprudential guidance in solving its political or public law problems than in solving those of private law. The organic document itself was novel in phrase and philosophy, and there was no judicial experience and no very persuasive body of learning to aid in the interpretation of the instrument. True, the Privy Council in colonial times may have dealt with analogous controversies as to the *ultra vires* character of colonial acts, or as to the powers of colonial governments under Royal Charters. But in the original states the people appear to have been highly sensitive about the newly acquired position of each state as a sovereign power, won by the treaty which recognized their independence: as parties to the federal compact the states were not the equivalent of chartered colonial corporations. Small wonder, then, that Marshall's great constitutional decisions cite no precedents, that they are argued out of political philosophy, and that later courts again and again have overruled outmoded doctrines and turned to new ones as political or economic conditions changed.

The question that the present times put into the minds of

thoughtful people is to what extent Supreme Court interpretations of the Constitution will or can preserve the free government of which the Court is a part. A cult of libertarian judicial
activists now assails the Court almost as bitterly for renouncing
power as the earlier "liberals" once did for assuming too much
power. This cult appears to believe that the Court can find in a
4,000-word eighteenth-century document or its nineteenth-century
Amendments, or can plausibly supply, some clear bulwark against
all dangers and evils that today beset us internally. This assumes
that the Court will be the dominant factor in shaping the constitutional practice of the future and can and will maintain, not
only equality with the elective branches, but a large measure of
supremacy and control over them. I may be biased against this
attitude because it is so contrary to the doctrines of the critics
of the Court, of whom I was one, at the time of the Roosevelt
proposal to reorganize the judiciary. But it seems to me a doctrine
wholly incompatible with faith in democracy, and in so far as it
encourages a belief that the judges may be left to correct the
result of public indifference to issues of liberty in choosing Presidents, Senators, and Representatives, it is a vicious teaching.

I shall pass over as not germane to my subject the question
whether the Constitution itself is adequate for the security problems, the economic problems, and the political problems of our
day. But I do not think that would be an academic question.
We face the rivalry, which may break into the hostility, of concentrated governments that can decide quickly and secretly on
their policies. Our power is so dispersed that nothing can be
decided quickly or secretly. But I assume the permanence of our
constitutional scheme, if for no other reason than our inability
to agree on any other. The difficulties of amendment are such
that many look to interpretation rather than amendment as a
means of change.

But before we take the measure of the values the Court should
and in some degree can protect, we must not overlook the things
now practically beyond its control. Two of the greatest powers
possessed by the political branches, which seem to me the
disaster-potentials in our system, are utterly beyond judicial reach.
These are the war power and the money, taxing, and spending
power, which is the power of inflation. The improvident use of
these powers can destroy the conditions for the existence of

liberty, because either can set up great currents of strife within the population which might carry down constitutional forms and limitations before them.

The Constitution made what in its day was a logical division of the war power, delegating to Congress the power to declare war and to the President, as Commander in Chief, the power to conduct it. But the twentieth century ushered in an era of undeclared wars and thereby drained much of the substance out of the congressional power to declare war. It is apparent now that the President can so handle foreign affairs and the armed forces as to leave Congress no real choice but to declare war or as to involve us in warfare without any declaration. Korea stands as an example of the actual concentration of the war power in the President. That wars and rumors of wars are the great threats to political stability and to liberty needs no demonstration. Total war means total subjection of the individual to the state. We may resist "creeping socialism" or the coming of the omnipotent socialized state in peacetime. But manpower, labor, property, material, profit, rent, and even food are subject to the planned economy and galloping socialism of modern war. This form of military socialization is accepted as patriotic, and dissenters are coerced into obedience. But it sets a pattern which is not easily changed when peace is restored, and it is no accident that the doctrines of Marx were sterile until the era of total wars and then took their deepest root in countries most deeply affected by war.

The other disaster-potential is the power over our money system and the power to tax and spend for the public welfare. In the famous Agricultural Adjustment Act case the political branches lost a case and won a cause. Even in holding that Act invalid, the Supreme Court adopted the Federalist view of the spending power and declared, "It results that the power of Congress to authorize expenditure of public moneys for public purposes is not limited by the direct grants of legislative power found in the Constitution." [12] The Court earlier had held that a suit by a federal taxpayer to restrain expenditures of public money on the ground that the controlling statute is invalid cannot be maintained and that a state may not institute such an action to protect her citizens.[13]

Thus the two disaster-potential powers are insulated from all judicial control—the war power practically in the hands of the

President, the spending power in the hands of Congress. Either improvidently used can bring catastrophe so extensive as to carry down with it all else that we value. War and inflation and their kin have released the evil forces which have destroyed liberty elsewhere. No protection against these catastrophic courses can be expected from the judiciary. The people must guard against these dangers at the polls.

The political function which the Supreme Court, more or less effectively, may be called upon to perform comes to this: In a society in which rapid changes tend to upset all equilibrium, the Court, without exceeding its own limited powers, must strive to maintain the great system of balances upon which our free government is based. Whether these balances and checks are essential to liberty elsewhere in the world is beside the point; they are indispensable to the society we know. Chief of these balances are: first, between the Executive and Congress; second, between the central government and the states; third, between state and state; fourth, between authority, be it state or national, and the liberty of the citizen, or between the rule of the majority and the rights of the individual.

I have said that in these matters the Court must respect the limitations on its own powers because judicial usurpation is to me no more justifiable and no more promising of permanent good to the country than any other kind. So I presuppose a Court that will not depart from the judicial process, will not go beyond resolving cases and controversies brought to it in conventional form, and will not consciously encroach upon the functions of its coordinate branches. Whether in case of a clearly unconstitutional usurpation of power by one of the other branches the Court would be justified in stepping out of its judicial role and itself exercising a usurped counterbalancing power, I do not stop to consider, because I think in such an event the judicial voice would be little heeded in the chaos.

EXECUTIVE V. LEGISLATIVE

It is hard to conceive a task more fundamentally political than to maintain amidst changing conditions the balance between the executive and legislative branches of our federal system. The Supreme Court often is required to arbitrate between the two because litigation in one form or another raises questions as to the legitimacy of the acts of one branch or the other under the doctrine of separation of powers. In such cases the Court has found no precedent from any other country or in the judicial interpretation of any similar written instrument, and it has had to devise its own doctrine from time to time.

The Court, both before and after the Roosevelt influence was felt in its appointments, has tended strongly to support the power of the President in matters involving foreign affairs.[14] On the other hand, where only internal affairs are involved, the Court has been more inclined to restrict executive power. It halted a presidential effort indirectly to control the policies of the administrative agencies by removal of a Federal Trade Commissioner.[15] In the cases striking down the NIRA, the Court refused to sanction the congressional practice of delegating power to the President to make codes for industry that would be the equivalent of new laws.[16] The Court has kept the Executive from usurping the adjudicative function through military trials of offenders by holding such trials illegal in *Ex parte Milligan,* 4 Wall. (71 U. S.) 2, after, however, they had been running riot for a number of years. In the more recent case of *United States ex rel. Quirin* v. *Cox,* 317 U. S. 1, the Court met in special session to review the legality of the conviction of the eight German saboteurs who had been tried by a military commission set up by President Roosevelt, although his proclamation and order of July 2, 1942, provided that they should not be privileged "to seek any remedy or maintain any proceeding directly or indirectly, or to have any such remedy or proceeding sought on their behalf, in the courts. . . ."[17] This part of the President's proclamation was quietly rejected and the saboteurs were given a full hearing, as a result of which, however, the trial was found to have been legal and the convictions were sustained.

In the more recent Steel Seizure case[18] the Court refused to sanction a presidential seizure of private property without congressional authorization, holding that the President has no such inherent power under the Constitution. But I felt constrained in that case to point out the inadequacies of judicial power to appraise or control the realistic balance of power between Congress and the President.[19] This is because of the gap that exists between the President's paper powers and his actual powers. The real potency of the Executive office does not show on the face of the Constitution. The relative influence of the President and of the Congress has fluctuated widely, depending on the personal and political strength of the particular President as compared with that of the congressional leadership. A Congress stampeded by a powerful leader like Thaddeus Stevens may cripple a President who is politically vulnerable, and a senatorial coalition may break the foreign policy of even an able and strong President like Wilson. On the other hand, a White House tenant who is a skillful manipulator of his extralegal influences may force an unwelcome program through Congress.

What are these sources of presidential strength? First, the Executive power is concentrated in a single head in whose choice the whole nation has a part, making him the focus of public hopes and expectations. No collection of local representatives can rival him in prestige. None can gain such ready and effective access to the modern means of communication with the masses or exert such influence on public opinion; this is one of his most effective leverages upon those in Congress who are supposed to balance his power. As the nation's activities have spread, the President wields the power of appointment and promotion over a vast multitude of our people. He is not merely the Chief Magistrate of the Republic; he is the titular and usually the actual head of the prevailing political party, whose loyalties and interest enable him to win as political leader what he could not command under the Constitution. Woodrow Wilson summed it all up in the observation that "if he rightly interpret the national thought and boldly insist upon it, he is irresistible. . . . His office is anything he has the sagacity and force to make it." [20]

Yet it depends not upon the President alone but upon his sagacity and force measured against that of the Congress as manifested in its leadership. If Congress forfeits the respect of the country, it will not be able to balance the power of the Executive. No matter what the Supreme Court opines, only Congress itself can keep its power from slipping through its fingers.

FEDERAL POWER V. STATE POWER

It is the maintenance of the constitutional equilibrium between the states and the Federal Government that has brought the most vexatious questions to the Supreme Court. That it was the duty of the Court, within its own constitutional functions, to preserve this balance has been asserted by the Court many times; that the Constitution is vague and ambiguous on this subject is shown by the history preceding our Civil War. It is undeniable that ever since that war ended we have been in a cycle of rapid centralization, and Court opinions have sanctioned a considerable concentration of power in the Federal Government with a corresponding diminution in the authority and prestige of state governments. Indeed, long ago an acute foreign observer declared the United States to be "a nation concealed under the form of a federation." [21] As respected an authority as Charles Evans Hughes declared nearly three decades ago that "far more important to the development of the country, than the decisions holding acts of Congress to be invalid, have been those in which the authority of Congress has been sustained and adequate national power to meet the necessities of a growing country has been found to exist within constitutional limitations." [22]

Here again the principal causes of this concentration have not been within judicial control. Improved methods of transportation and communication; the increasing importance of foreign affairs and of interstate commerce; the absorption of revenue sources by the nation with the consequent appeal by distressed localities directly to Washington for relief and work projects, bypassing the state entirely; the direct election of Senators; and various other factors—all have contributed to move the center of gravity from the state capital to that of the nation.

I think it is a mistake to lump all states' rights together as is done so frequently in political discussions.

There can be no doubt that in the original Constitution the states surrendered to the Federal Government the power to regulate interstate commerce, or commerce among the states. They did so in the light of a disastrous experience in which commerce and prosperity were reduced to the vanishing point by states discriminating against each other through devices of regulation, taxation and exclusion. It is more important today than it was then that we remain one commercial and economic unit and not a collection of parasitic states preying upon each other's commerce. I make no concealment of and offer no apology for my philosophy that the federal interstate commerce power should be strongly supported and that the impingement of the states upon that commerce which moves among them should be restricted to narrow limits.

It was early perceived that to allow the Federal Government to spend money for internal improvements would aggrandize its powers as against those of the states. It was not until the famous decision holding the Social Security Act constitutional that this controversy over the federal power to tax and spend for the general welfare was settled, and settled in favor of the existence of that power in the Federal Government.[23] I believe that this controversy was rightly settled, but there is no denying that the power is vast and, uncontrolled, leads to the invasion of sources of revenue and builds up the Federal Government by creating organizations to make the expenditures. But here we are dealing with powers granted to the Federal Government, if not entirely without ambiguity, at least in language which fairly admits of the construction given it and which fairly warned those who adopted the Constitution that such results might follow.

Considerations of a different nature arise from interferences with states' rights under the vague and ambiguous mandate of the Fourteenth Amendment. The legislative history of that Amendment is not enlightening, and the history of its ratification is not edifying. I shall not go into the controversy as to whether the Fourteenth Amendment, by a process of incorporation or impregnation, directs against the states prohibitions found in the earlier Amendments. Whether it does or not, I think the Fourteenth Amendment has been considerably abused.

For more than half a century the Supreme Court found in the Fourteenth Amendment authority for striking down various social experiments by the states. The history of judicial nullification of state social and economic legislation is too well known to justify repetition here. It came to its culmination when the Court wound up the October 1935 Term by declaring that there was no power in either state or nation to enact a minimum wage law,[24] a position repudiated within a few months by the conventions of both political parties and retracted by the Court itself with some haste. That retraction probably brought an end to the use of the Fourteenth Amendment to prevent experiments by the states with economic and social and labor legislation.

The states have probably been more venturesome and radical in their experimentation than the Congress. This is perhaps explainable by the fact that their experiments are more easily modified if unsuccessful. In the Granger movement and in the social legislation that followed it the states took the lead. On the other hand, they have enacted more extreme legislation for the control and restriction of labor unions when the tide ran the other way. In each instance the interest adversely affected has sought to obtain a holding that due process of law prevented the state from controlling its affairs and also prevented the nation from interfering, thus disabling either from exerting effective control. It is my basic view that whenever any organization or combination of individuals, whether in a corporation, a labor union or other body, obtains such economic or legal advantage that it can control or in effect govern the lives of other people, it is subject to the control of the Government, be it state or federal, for the Government can suffer no rivals in the field of coercion. Liberty requires that coercion be applied to the individual not by other individuals but by the Government after full inquiry into the justification.

Today, however, we have a different application of the Fourteenth Amendment. Today it is being used not to restrain state legislatures but to set aside the acts of state courts, particularly in criminal matters. This practice has proceeded to a point where the federal courts are in acute controversy with the state courts, and the assembled Chief Justices of the state courts have adopted severe resolutions condemning the federal intervention. I must say that I am rather in sympathy with the Chief Justices of the state courts on this subject. I believe we are unjustifiably invading the rights of the states by expanding the constitutional concept of due process to include the idea that the error of a trial court deprives it of "jurisdiction," [25] by including in the concept by interpretation all other constitutional provisions not literally incorporated in the Fourteenth Amendment, and, in the alternative, by incorporating into it all of our ideas of decency, even to the point of making a constitutional issue of rulings upon evidence.

The Court has been drawing into the federal system more and more control by federal agencies over local police agencies. I have no doubt that the latter are often guilty of serious invasions of individual rights. But there are more fundamental questions involved in the interpretation of the antiquated, cumbersome, and vague civil rights statutes which give the Department of Justice the right to prosecute state officials.[26] If the Department of Justice must prosecute local officials, the FBI must investigate them, and no local agency which is subject to federal investigation, inspection, and discipline is a free agency. I cannot say that our country could have no central police without becoming totalitarian, but I can say with great conviction that it cannot become totalitarian without a centralized national police. At his trial Hermann Goering, with great candor, related the steps by which the Nazi party obtained complete domination of Germany, and one of the first was the establishment of the supremacy of the national over the local police authorities. So it was in Russia, and so it has been in every totalitarian state. All that is necessary is to have a national police competent to investigate all manner of offenses, and then, in the parlance of the street, it will have enough on enough people, even if it does not elect to prosecute them, so that it will find no opposition to its policies. Even those who are supposed to supervise it are likely to fear it. I believe that the safeguard of our liberty lies in limiting any national policing or investigative organization, first of all to a small number of strictly federal offenses, and secondly to nonpolitical ones. The fact that we may have confidence in the administration of a federal investigative agency under its existing heads does not mean that it may not revert again to the days when the Department of Justice was headed by men to whom the investigatory power was a weapon to be used for their own purposes.

It is a difficult question and always will remain a debatable question where, in particular instances, federal due process should step into state court proceedings and set them aside. When the state courts render harsh or unconsidered judgments, they invite this power to be used. But I think in the long run the transgressions of liberty by the Federal Government, with its all-powerful organization, are much more to be feared than those of the several states, which have a greater capacity for self-correction.

STATE V. STATE

Another clearly political type of litigation is that of state against state. It was logical that in a federation the different units should have some arbiter to settle their differences. Congress was made a supervisor of their separate compacts or agreements. The Supreme Court was made the arbiter of their controversies. Here was the precedent for an international court, for the states waived their sovereignty sufficiently to submit to a compulsory jurisdiction over their controversies with each other. This seems a hopeful precedent for an alternative to war and chaos and reprisals. Under this head of jurisdiction the Court has settled boundary disputes,[27] apportioned the debts of a divided state between the two new divisions,[28] and determined many disputes over rivers and waters.[29]

To what source may the Court look for law to govern such controversies? The actual practice perhaps is well illustrated in Mr. Justice Cardozo's opinion in *New Jersey* v. *Delaware*, 291 U. S. 361. His search carried him through many ancient documents, which he interpreted according to the common law of property, and he compared the claims of the two states in the light of that body of learning. But this was inadequate for the solution of the case and resort was had to international law. He traced international law through the Court's own decisions and through all of the conventional authorities, American and foreign. He found international law inconclusive and no positive law applicable. He declared that "International law, or the law that governs between states, has at times, like the common law within states, a twilight existence during which it is hardly distinguishable from morality or justice, till at length the *imprimatur* of a court attests its jural quality." [30] He concluded that in these circumstances it was within the power of the judicial process to develop and apply a formula consonant with justice and with the political and social needs of the interstate or international legal system. Reduced to its simplest terms, what the Court seemed to be saying in that case was that it found no controlling law and was obliged to declare some, in the light of the experience and learning of the law in similar situations. The Court has no escape in many cases of this character from the undesirable alternatives of refusing to obey its duty to decide the case or of devising some rule of decision which has no precedent or positive law authority.

I know that it is now regarded as more or less provincial and reactionary to cite the Tenth Amendment, which reserves to the states and the people the powers not delegated to the Federal

Government. That Amendment is rarely mentioned in judicial opinions, rarely cited in argument. But our forefathers made it a part of the Bill of Rights in order to retain in the localities certain powers and not to allow them to drift into centralized hands. Perhaps the Tenth Amendment is drifting into oblivion as constitutional provisions may sometimes do. . . .

MAJORITY V. INDIVIDUAL

Perhaps the most delicate, difficult and shifting of all balances which the Court is expected to maintain is that between liberty and authority. It is not so easy as some people believe to determine what serves liberty best by way of restriction of authority. For example, the removal of the Japanese from the West Coast during the War, which seemed to me plainly unconstitutional as applied to citizens, was rationalized as a service to ultimate liberty.[31] And I suppose no one would be more likely than Abraham Lincoln to win recognition by common vote as the greatest servant of freedom; yet President Lincoln, at the outset of his administration, suspended the writ of habeas corpus and resorted to wholesale arrest without warrant, detention without trial, and imprisonment without judicial conviction. Private mail was opened, and Cabinet officers simply sent telegrams ordering persons to be arrested and held without communication or counsel. The power was given to generals of various of the northern states to suppress newspapers and suspend the writ. President Lincoln, in his famous letter to Erastus Corning and others, defended his conduct, saying all that ever could be said and what always will be said in favor of such policies in time of emergency.[32] Those policies were sharply but unavailingly condemned in May of 1861 by the aged Chief Justice Taney, and he has said all that can be said on the other side.[33] Had Mr. Lincoln scrupulously observed the Taney policy, I do not know whether we would have had any liberty, and had the Chief Justice adopted Mr. Lincoln's philosophy as the philosophy of the law, I again do not know whether we would have had any liberty.

Lord Acton has said that liberty is a term of two hundred definitions.[34] About all I am sure of is that it is something never established for the future, but something which each age must provide for itself. I think we are given the rough outlines of a free society by our Bill of Rights. Liberty is not the mere absence of restraint, it is not a spontaneous product of majority rule, it is not achieved merely by lifting underprivileged classes to power, nor is it the inevitable by-product of technological expansion. It is achieved only by a rule of law.

But we must bear in mind that in the protection of individual or minority rights, we are often impinging on the principle of majority rule. Judicial opinions rarely face this dilemma. Let us take, for example, a community engaged largely in steel work, many of whose inhabitants are employed on night shifts and get their rest by day. Acting through regularly chosen representatives, the municipality duly enacts a regulation that precludes doorbell ringing in the distribution of literature or goods. A religious faction insists upon ringing doorbells to summon the occupant to the door to receive religious tracts that attack his religion and seek to convert him to the faith of the caller. If the Court holds that the right of free speech includes the right to enter upon private property and summon the owner to the door, it necessarily holds that a majority of a community are without the right to protect their hours of rest against such religiously inspired aggression.

In case after case in which so-called civil rights are involved, the question simmers down to one of the extent to which majority rule will be set aside. This issue has been debated,[35] but it has by no means been settled, and views shift as the occasion for judicial intervention shifts from case to case. About all we need to note, unless we were to go into a lengthy discussion of the particular cases of application of the power, is that the power of the Court to protect individual or minority rights has on the other side of the coin the power to restrain the majority. Some profound political philosophers, among them Mr. Jefferson, doubted the advisability of such intervention. Mr. Jefferson asked where else we may "find the origin of *just* powers, if not in the majority of the society? Will it be in the minority? Or in an individual of that minority?" [36] Perhaps we should say that it is only to be found in the law, in rationally and dispassionately devised rules which limit the majority's control over the individual and the minority. But even with the best draftsmanship possible such rules cannot but leave many questions for interpretation.

Moreover, we must remember that the Supreme Court is not the only force that is operating upon the Constitution. Custom, even in most vital matters, may serve to alter it. I suppose the election of a President is the most decisive and important recurring event in our national life. Nothing concerned the forefathers more, and they set up an elaborate and original system to assure nonpartisan, deliberative choice from among all the citizens by electors selected for their leadership and judgment. This system has been suffocated by custom. The American public now sits at its television, entertained by the antics of two national conventions which limit their practicable choice of President to two men. Neither of these conventions nor the parties holding them has the slightest recognition in the Constitution, whose framers took every precaution to prevent the emergence of parties.

The Supreme Court, in the exercise of its power, has repeatedly come into collision with the strong executives of the nation. Jefferson, Jackson, Lincoln, and Franklin Roosevelt have been in open conflict with it. The clash has occurred where the Court was believed to be entering political realms through the passageway of private litigation. It would serve no purpose to review the merits of the conflict here, but in almost every instance it has occurred in such form as really to raise the question of minority and individual rights against majority rule: in each instance the President has been the representative of a powerful, popular majority. This is one of the great dilemmas of judicial power and one most avoided in discussion of the subject. So far as I can see, nothing has been accomplished in any of the controversies to settle or put at rest the questions which cause them. Judicial power to nullify a law duly passed by the representative process is a restriction upon the power of the majority to govern the country. Unrestricted majority rule leaves the individual in the minority unprotected. This is the dilemma and you have to take your choice. The Constitution-makers made their choice in favor of a limited majority rule.

In interpreting that limitation, of course, the Supreme Court from time to time makes and alters the law of the Constitution. It is idle to say that this is merely the ordinary process of private law interpretation. When the Court goes too far in interfering with the processes of the majority, it will again encounter a drive against its power or personnel. The power which has been exerted by the Court and which lies at the root of the controversies with the Executive has no more been renounced by the post-

Roosevelt Court than it was by the pre-Roosevelt Court, though the lack of novel and progressive legislation has offered less occasion for its exercise. My philosophy has been and continues to be that such an institution, functioning by such methods, cannot and should not try to seize the initiative in shaping the policy of the law, either by constitutional interpretation or by statutory construction. While the line to be drawn between interpretation and legislation is difficult, and numerous dissents turn upon it, there is a limit beyond which the Court incurs the just charge of trying to supersede the law-making branches. Every Justice has been accused of legislating and every one has joined in that accusation of others. When the Court has gone too far, it has provoked reactions which have set back the cause it is designed to advance, and has sometimes called down upon itself severe rebuke.

If an organized society wants the kind of justice that an independent, professional judicial establishment is qualified to administer, our judiciary is certainly a most effective instrument for applying law and justice to individual cases and for cultivating public attitudes which rely upon law and seek justice. But I know of no modern instance in which any judiciary has saved a whole people from the great currents of intolerance, passion, usurpation, and tyranny which have threatened liberty and free institutions. The Dred Scott decision did not settle the question of the power to end slavery, and I very much doubt that had Mr. Justice McLean not dissented in that case it would have done any more to avoid war. No court can support a reactionary regime and no court can innovate or implement a new one. I doubt that any court, whatever its powers, could have saved Louis XVI or Marie Antoinette. None could have avoided the French Revolution, none could have stopped its excesses, and none could have prevented its culmination in the dictatorship of Napoleon. In Germany a courageous court refused to convict those whom the Nazi government sought to make the scapegoats for the Reichstag fire, clandestinely set by the Nazis themselves, and other courts decreed both the Nazi and the Communist parties to be illegal under German law. Those judgments fell on deaf ears and became dead letters because the political forces at the time were against them.

It is not idle speculation to inquire which comes first, either in time or importance, an independent and enlightened judiciary or a free and tolerant society. Must we first maintain a system of free political government to assure a free judiciary, or can we rely on an aggressive, activist judiciary to guarantee free government? While each undoubtedly is a support for the other, and the two are frequently found together, it is my belief that the attitude of a society and of its organized political forces, rather than its legal machinery, is the controlling force in the character of free institutions.

I am a fairly consistent reader of British newspapers. I have been repeatedly impressed with the speed and certainty with which the slightest invasion of British individual freedom or minority rights by officials of the government is picked up in Parliament, not merely by the opposition but by the party in power, and made the subject of persistent questioning, criticism, and sometimes rebuke. There is no waiting on the theory that the judges will take care of it. In this country, on the contrary, we rarely have a political issue made of any kind of invasion of civil liberty. On the contrary, district attorneys who have been rebuked by the courts are frequently promoted by the public. The attitude seems to be, leave it to the judges. Years after the event takes place, the judges make their pronouncement, often in the form of letting some admittedly guilty person go, and that ends the matter. In Great Britain, to observe civil liberties is good politics and to transgress the rights of the individual or the minority is bad politics. In the United States, I cannot say that this is so. Whether the political conscience is relieved because the responsibility here is made largely a legal one, I cannot say, but of this I am sure: any court which undertakes by its legal processes to enforce civil liberties needs the support of an enlightened and vigorous public opinion which will be intelligent and discriminating as to what cases really are civil liberties cases and what questions really are involved in those cases. I do not think the American public is enlightened on this subject.

Sometimes one is tempted to quote his former self, not only to pay his respects to the author but to demonstrate the consistency of his views, if not their correctness. On the 150th anniversary of the Supreme Court, speaking for the executive branch of the Government as Attorney General, I said to the Justices:

"However well the Court and its bar may discharge their tasks, the destiny of this Court is inseparably linked to the fate of our democratic system of representative government. Judicial functions, as we have evolved them, can be discharged only in that kind of society which is willing to submit its conflicts to adjudication and to subordinate power to reason. The future of the Court may depend more upon the competence of the executive and legislative branches of government to solve their problems adequately and in time than upon the merit which is its own." [37]

REFERENCES

[1] The statement was a personal one made to Mr. Justice Jackson and is recorded in Jackson, *Full Faith and Credit*, p. 2 (1945).

[2] E.g., *Cochran v. Louisiana State Board*, 281 U. S. 370; *Mountain Timber Co. v. Washington*, 243 U. S. 219; *Pacific States Telephone & Telegraph Co. v. Oregon*, 223 U. S. 118.

[3] E.g., *Coleman v. Miller*, 307 U. S. 433; *Leser v. Garnett*, 258 U. S. 130; *Luther v. Borden*, 7 How. (48 U. S.) 1.

[4] E.g., *Field v. Clark*, 143 U. S. 649; *Harwood v. Wentworth*, 162 U. S. 547; *Flint v. Stone Tracy Co.*, 220 U. S. 107, 143.

[5] E.g., *Ludecke v. Watkins*, 335 U. S. 160; *Commercial Trust Co. v. Miller*, 262 U. S. 51. Cf. *Woods v. Cloyd W. Miller Co.*, 333 U. S. 138, 146 (concurring opinion).

[6] E.g., *Clark v. Allen*, 331 U. S. 503; *Terlinden v. Ames*, 184 U. S. 270; *Doe v. Braden*, 16 How. (57 U. S.) 635.

[7] E.g., *United States v. Pink*, 315 U. S. 203; *Oetjen v. Central Leather Co.*, 246 U. S. 297; *Kennett v. Chambers*, 14 How. (55 U. S.) 38.

[8] E.g., *Harisiades v. Shaughnessy*, 342 U. S. 580; *Chicago & Southern Air Lines, Inc. v. Waterman S.S. Corp.*, 333 U. S. 103; *In re Cooper*, 143 U. S. 472; *Foster v. Neilson*, 2 Pet. (27 U. S.) 253.

[9] E.g., *Wood v. Broom*, 287 U. S. 1; *Colegrove v. Green*, 328 U. S. 549; *Anderson v. Jordan*, 343 U. S. 912.

[10] E.g., *MacDougall v. Green*, 335 U. S. 281; *Illinois ex rel. Sankstone v. Jarecki*, 346 U. S. 861; *White v. Howard*, 347 U. S. 910.

[11] E.g., *Cook v. Fortson, Turman v. Duckworth*, 329 U. S. 675; *South v. Peters*, 339 U. S. 276.

[12] *United States v. Butler*, 297 U. S. 1, 66.

[13] *Massachusetts v. Mellon*, 262 U. S. 447.

[14] E.g., *United States v. Curtiss-Wright Export Corp.*, 299 U. S. 304; *Chicago & Southern Air Lines, Inc. v. Watermann S.S. Corp.*, 253 U. S. 103.

[15] *Humphrey's Executor v. United States*, 295 U. S. 602.

[16] *Panama Refining Co. v. Ryan*, 293 U. S. 388; *A.L.A. Schechter Poultry Corp. v. United States*, 295 U. S. 495.

[17] Proclamation 2561, 7 Fed. Reg. 5101.

[18] *Youngstown Sheet & Tube Co. v. Sawyer*, 343 U. S. 579.

[19] *Id.*, at 634 (concurring opinion).

[20] Wilson, *Constitutional Government in the United States*, 68, 69 (1911).

[21] Dicey, *Law of the Constitution*, App. 604. (9th ed. 1939).

[22] Hughes, *The Supreme Court of the United States*, 96 (1928).

[23] *Helvering v. Davis*, 301 U. S. 619.

[24] *Morehead* v. *New York ex rel. Tipaldo*, 298 U. S. 587.

[25] *Johnson* v. *Zerbst*, 304 U. S. 458, 467-468; see also *Brown* v. *Allen*, 344 U. S. 443, 532 (concurring opinion). [Mr. Justice Jackson had written "Johnson" next to this note.]

[26] See *Screws* v. *United States*, 325 U. S. 91.

[27] E.g., *Maryland* v. *West Virginia*, 217 U. S. 1; *Indiana* v. *Kentucky*, 163 U. S. 520; *Missouri* v. *Iowa*, 7 How. (48 U. S.) 660.

[28] *Virginia* v. *West Virginia*, 206 U. S. 290.

[29] E.g., *New Jersey* v. *Delaware*, 291 U. S. 361; *Wisconsin* v. *Illinois*, 278 U. S. 367; *Kansas* v. *Colorado*, 206 U. S. 46.

[30] 291 U. S., at 383.

[31] *Korematsu* v. *United States*, 323 U. S. 214.

[32] VIII *Complete Works of Abraham Lincoln* (ed. Nicolay and Hay), 298 (c. 1894).

[33] *Ex parte Merryman*, Reports of Cases at Law and Equity and in the Admiralty determined in the Circuit Court of the United States for the District of Maryland by Roger Brooke Taney, 246 (1871).

[34] Acton, *Essays on Freedom and Power*, 14 (1948).

[35] *West Virginia State Board of Education* v. *Barnette*, 319 U. S. 624.

[36] Letter to Major John Cartwright, June 5, 1824, VII *Writings of Thomas Jefferson* (ed. Washington), 356 (1861).

[37] 309 U. S. v, vii.

HUGO BLACK
ASSOCIATE JUSTICE, 1937—

Absolutes, Courts, and the Bill of Rights*

. . . What is a bill of rights? In the popular sense it is any document setting forth the liberties of the people. I prefer to think of our Bill of Rights as including all provisions of the original Constitution and Amendments that protect individual liberty by barring government from acting in a particular area or from acting except under certain prescribed procedures. I have in mind such clauses in the body of the Constitution itself as those which safeguard the right of habeas corpus, forbid bills of attainder and *ex post facto* laws, guarantee trial by jury, and strictly define treason and limit the way it can be tried and punished. I would certainly add to this list the last constitutional prohibition in Article Six that "no religious Test shall ever be required as a qualification to any Office or public Trust under the United States."

I shall speak to you about the Bill of Rights only as it bears on powers of the Federal Government. . . .

In applying the Bill of Rights to the Federal Government there is today a sharp difference of views as to how far its provisions should be held to limit the law-making power of Congress. How this difference is finally resolved will, in my judgment, have far-reaching consequences upon our liberties. I shall first summarize what those different views are.

Some people regard the prohibitions of the Constitution, even its most unequivocal commands, as mere admonitions which

* From the James Madison Lecture, "The Bill of Rights," New York University School of Law, New York, N. Y., February 17, 1960. Printed in 35 *New York Univ. Law Review* 865 (1960). Reprinted by permission of Mr. Justice Black and the publisher.

Congress need not always observe. This viewpoint finds many different verbal expressions. For example, it is sometimes said that Congress may abridge a constitutional right if there is a clear and present danger that the free exercise of the right will bring about a substantive evil that Congress has authority to prevent. Or it is said that a right may be abridged where its exercise would cause so much injury to the public that this injury would outweigh the injury to the individual who is deprived of the right. Again, it is sometimes said that the Bill of Rights' guarantees must "compete" for survival against general powers expressly granted to Congress, and that the individual's right must, if outweighed by the public interest, be subordinated to the Government's competing interest in denying the right. All of these formulations, and more with which you are doubtless familiar, rest, at least in part, on the premise that there are no "absolute" prohibitions in the Constitution, and that all constitutional problems are questions of reasonableness, proximity, and degree. This view comes close to the English doctrine of legislative omnipotence, qualified only by the possibility of a judicial veto if the Supreme Court finds that a congressional choice between "competing" policies has no reasonable basis.

I cannot accept this approach to the Bill of Rights. It is my belief that there *are* "absolutes" in our Bill of Rights, and that they were put there on purpose by men who knew what words meant, and meant their prohibitions to be "absolutes." The whole history and background of the Constitution and Bill of Rights, as I understand it, belies the assumption or conclusion that our ultimate constitutional freedoms are no more than our English ancestors had when they came to this new land to get new freedoms. The historical and practical purposes of a Bill of Rights, the very use of a written constitution, indigenous to America, the language the Framers used, the kind of three-department government they took pains to set up, all point to the creation of a government which was denied all power to do some things under any and all circumstances, and all power to do other things except precisely in the manner prescribed. In this talk I will state some of the reasons why I hold this view. In doing so, however, I shall not attempt to discuss the wholly different and complex problem of the marginal scope of each individual amendment as applied to the particular facts of particular cases. For example, there is a question as to whether the First Amendment was intended to protect speech that courts find "obscene." I shall not stress this or similar differences of construction, nor shall I add anything to the views I expressed in the recent case of *Smith* v. *California*, 361 U. S. 147, 155. I am primarily discussing here whether liberties *admittedly* covered by the Bill of Rights can nevertheless be abridged on the ground that a superior public interest justifies the abridgment. I think the Bill of Rights made its safeguards superior.

Today most Americans seem to have forgotten the ancient evils which forced their ancestors to flee to this new country and to form a government stripped of old powers used to oppress them. But the Americans who supported the Revolution and the adoption of our Constitution knew firsthand the dangers of tyrannical governments. They were familiar with the long existing practice of English persecutions of people wholly because of their religious or political beliefs. They knew that many accused of such offenses had stood, helpless to defend themselves, before biased legislators and judges.

John Lilburne, a Puritan dissenter, is a conspicuous example. He found out the hard way that a citizen of England could not get a court and jury trial under English law if Parliament wanted to try and punish him in some kind of summary and unfair method of its own. Time and time again, when his religious or political activities resulted in criminal charges against him, he had demanded jury trials, under the "law of the land" but had been refused. Due to "trials" either by Parliament, its legislative committees, or courts subservient to the King or to Parliament, against all of which he vigorously protested as contrary to "due process," or "the law of the land," Lilburne had been whipped, put in the pillory, sent to prison, heavily fined and banished from England, all its islands and dominions, under penalty of death should he return. This last sentence was imposed by a simple Act of Parliament, without any semblance of a trial. Upon his defiant return he was arrested and subjected to an unfair trial for his life. His chief defense was that the Parliamentary conviction was a nullity, as a denial of "due process of law," which he claimed was guaranteed under Magna Charta, the 1628 Petition of Right, and statutes passed to carry them out. He also challenged the power of Parliament to enact bills of attainder on the same grounds—due process of law. Lilburne repeatedly and vehemently contended that he was entitled to notice, and indictment, and court trial by jury under the known laws of England; that he had a right to be represented by counsel; that he had a right to have witnesses summoned in his behalf and be confronted by the witnesses against him; that he could not be compelled to testify against himself. When Lilburne finally secured a jury it courageously acquitted him, after which the jury itself was severely punished by the Court.

Prompted largely by the desire to save Englishmen from such legislative mockeries of fair trials, Lilburne and others strongly advocated adoption of an "Agreement of the People" which contained most of the provisions of our present Bill of Rights. That Agreement would have done away with Parliamentary omnipotence. Lilburne pointed out that the basic defect of Magna Charta and statutes conplementing it was that they were not binding on Parliament since "that which is done by one Parliament, as a Parliament, may be undone by the next Parliament; but an Agreement of the People begun and ended amongst the people can never come justly within the Parliament's cognizance to destroy." The proposed "Agreement of the People," Lilburne argued, could be changed only by the people and would bind Parliament as the supreme "law of the land." This same idea was picked up before the adoption of our Federal Constitution by Massachusetts and New Hampshire, which adopted their constitutions only after popular referendums. Our Federal Constitution is largely attributable to the same current of thinking.

Unfortunately, our own colonial history also provided ample reasons for people to be afraid to vest too much power in the national government. There had been bills of attainder here; women had been convicted and sentenced to death as "witches"; Quakers, Baptists and various Protestant sects had been persecuted from time to time. Roger Williams left Massachusetts to breathe the free air of new Rhode Island. Catholics were barred from holding office in many places. Test oaths were required in some of the colonies to bar any but Christians from holding office. In New England Quakers suffered death for their faith. Baptists went to jail in Virginia for preaching, which caused Madison, while a very young man, to deplore what he called that "diabolical hell-conceived principle of persecution." [1]

In the light of history, therefore, it is not surprising that when our Constitution was adopted without specific provisions to safeguard cherished individual rights from invasion by the legislative, as well as the executive and judicial departments of the National Government, a loud and irresistible clamor went up throughout the country. These protests were so strong that the Constitution was ratified by the very narrowest of votes in some of the states. It has been said, and I think correctly, that had there been no general agreement that a supplementary Bill of Rights would be adopted as soon as possible after Congress met, the Constitution would not have been ratified. It seems clear that this widespread demand for a Bill of Rights was due to a common fear of political and religious persecution should the national legislative power be left unrestrained as it was in England.

The form of government which was ordained and established in 1789 contains certain unique features which reflected the Framers' fear of arbitrary government and which clearly indicate an intention absolutely to limit what Congress could do. The first of these features is that our Constitution is written in a single document. Such constitutions are familiar today and it is not always remembered that our country was the first to have one. Certainly one purpose of a written constitution is to define and therefore more specifically limit government powers. An all-powerful government that can act as it pleases wants no such constitution—unless to fool the people. England had no written constitution and this once proved a source of tyranny, as our ancestors well knew. Jefferson said about this departure from the English type of government: "Our peculiar security is in the possession of a written Constitution. Let us not make it a blank paper by construction." [2]

A second unique feature of our Government is a Constitution supreme over the legislature. In England, statutes, Magna Charta and later declarations of rights had for centuries limited the power of the King, but they did not limit the power of Parliament. Although commonly referred to as a constitution, they were never the "supreme law of the land" in the way in which our Constitution is, much to the regret of statesmen like Pitt the elder. Parliament could change this English "Constitution"; Congress cannot change ours. Ours can only be changed by amendments ratified by three-fourths of the states. It was one of the great achievements of our Constitution that it ended legislative omnipotence here and placed all departments and agencies of government under one supreme law.

A third feature of our Government expressly designed to limit its powers was the division of authority into three coordinate branches none of which was to have supremacy over the others. This separation of powers with the checks and balances which each branch was given over the others was designed to prevent any branch, including the legislative, from infringing individual liberties safeguarded by the Constitution.

Finally, our Constitution was the first to provide a really independent judiciary. Moreover, as the Supreme Court held in *Marbury* v. *Madison*, 1 Cranch 137, correctly, I believe, this judiciary has the power to hold legislative enactments void that are repugnant to the Constitution and the Bill of Rights. In this country the judiciary was made independent because it has, I believe, the primary responsibility and duty of giving force and effect to constitutional liberties and limitations upon the executive and legislative branches. Judges in England were not always independent and they could not hold parliamentary acts void. Consequently, English courts could not be counted on to protect the liberties of the people against invasion by the Parliament, as many unfortunate Englishmen found out, such as Sir Walter Raleigh, who was executed as the result of an unfair trial, and a lawyer named William Prynne, whose ears were first cut off by court order and who subsequently, by another court order, had his remaining ear stumps gouged out while he was on a pillory. Prynne's offenses were writing books and pamphlets.

All of the unique features of our Constitution show an underlying purpose to create a new kind of limited government. Central to all of the Framers of the Bill of Rights was the idea that since government, particularly the national government newly created, is a powerful institution, its officials—all of them—must be compelled to exercise their powers within strictly defined boundaries. As Madison told Congress, the Bill of Rights' limitations point "sometimes against the abuse of the Executive power, sometimes against the Legislative, and in some cases against the community itself; or, in other words, against the majority in favor of the minority." [3] In the same speech Madison also explained that his proposed amendments were intended "to limit and qualify the powers of Government, by excepting out of the grant of power those cases in which the Government ought not to act, or to act only in a particular mode." In the light of this purpose let us now turn to the language of the first ten amendments to consider whether their provisions were written as mere admonitions to Congress or as absolute commands, proceeding for convenience from the last to the first.

The last two Amendments, the Ninth and Tenth, are general in character, but both emphasize the limited nature of the Federal Government. Number Ten restricts federal power to what the Constitution delegates to the central government, reserving all other powers to the states or to the people. Number Nine attempts to make certain that enumeration of some rights must "not be construed to deny or disparage others retained by the people." The use of the words, "the people," in both these Amendments strongly emphasizes the desire of the Framers to protect individual liberty.

The Seventh Amendment states that "In suits at common law, where the value in controversy shall exceed twenty-dollars, the right of trial by jury shall be preserved. . . ." This language clearly requires that jury trials must be afforded in the type of cases the Amendment describes. The Amendment goes on in equally unequivocal words to command that "no fact tried by a jury, shall be otherwise re-examined in any Court of the United States, than according to the rules of the common law."

Amendments Five, Six, and Eight relate chiefly to the procedures that government must follow when bringing its powers to bear against any person with a view to depriving him of his life, liberty, or property.

The Eighth Amendment forbids "excessive bail," "excessive fines," or the infliction of "cruel or unusual punishments." This is one of the less precise provisions. The courts are required to determine the meaning of such general terms as "excessive" and "unusual." But surely that does not mean that admittedly "excessive bail," "excessive fines," or "cruel punishments" could be justified on the ground of a "competing" public interest in carrying out some generally granted power like that given Congress to regulate commerce.

Amendment Six provides that in a criminal prosecution an accused shall have a "speedy and public trial, by an impartial jury of the State and district wherein the crime shall have been committed, which district shall have been previously ascertained by law, and to be informed of the nature and cause of the accusation; to be confronted with the witnesses against him; to have compulsory process for obtaining witnesses in his favor, and have the Assistance of Counsel for his defense." All of these requirements are cast in terms both definite and absolute. Trial by jury was also guaranteed in the original Constitution. The additions here, doubtless prompted by English trials of Americans away from their homes, are that a trial must be "speedy and public," "by an impartial jury," and in a district which "shall have been previously ascertained by law." If there is any one thing that is certain it is that the Framers intended both in the original Constitution and in the Sixth Amendment that persons charged with crime by the Federal Government had a right to be tried by jury. Suppose juries began acquitting people Congress thought should be convicted. Could Congress then provide some other form of trial, say by an administrative agency, or the military, where convictions could be more readily and certainly obtained, if it thought the safety of the nation so required? How about secret trials? By *partial* juries? Can it be that these are not absolute prohibitions?

The Sixth Amendment requires notice of the cause of an accusation, confrontation by witnesses, compulsory process and assistance of counsel. The experience of centuries has demonstrated the value of these procedures to one on trial for crime. And this Amendment purports to guarantee them by clear language. But if there are no absolutes in the Bill of Rights, these guarantees too can be taken away by Congress on findings that a competing public interest requires that defendants be tried without notice, without witnesses, without confrontation, and without counsel.

The Fifth Amendment provides:

No person shall be held to answer for a capital, or otherwise infamous crime, unless on a presentment or indictment of a Grand Jury, except in cases arising in the land or naval forces, or in the Militia, when in actual service in time of War or public danger; nor shall any person be subject for the same offence to be twice put in jeopardy of life or limb; nor shall be compelled in any criminal case to be a witness against himself, nor be deprived of life, liberty, or property, without due process of law; nor shall private property be taken for public use, without just compensation.

Most of these Fifth Amendment prohibitions are both definite and unequivocal. There has been much controversy about the meaning of "due process of law." Whatever its meaning, however, there can be no doubt that it must be granted. Moreover, few doubt that it has an historical meaning which denies Government the right to take away life, liberty, or property without trials properly conducted according to the Constitution and laws validly made in accordance with it. This, at least, was the meaning of "due process of law" when used in Magna Charta and other old English Statutes where it was referred to as "the law of the land."

The Fourth Amendment provides:

The right of the people to be secure in their persons, houses, papers, and effects, against unreasonable searches and seizures, shall not be violated, and no Warrants shall issue, but upon probable cause, supported by Oath or affirmation, and particularly describing the place to be searched, and the persons or things to be seized.

The use of the word "unreasonable" in this Amendment means, of course, that not *all* searches and seizures are prohibited. Only those which are *unreasonable* are unlawful. There may be much difference of opinion about whether a particular search or seizure is unreasonable and therefore forbidden by this Amendment. But if it *is* unreasonable, it is absolutely prohibited.

Likewise, the provision which forbids warrants for arrest, search or seizure without "probable cause" is itself an absolute prohibition.

The Third Amendment provides that:

No Soldier shall, in time of peace be quartered in any house, without the consent of the owner, nor in time of war, but in a manner to be prescribed by law.

Americans had recently suffered from the quartering of British troops in their homes, and so this Amendment is written in language that apparently no one has ever thought could be violated on the basis of an overweighing public interest.

Amendment Two provides that:

A well regulated militia, being necessary to the security of a free
State, the right of the people to keep and bear Arms, shall not be
infringed.

Although the Supreme Court has held this Amendment to include only arms necessary to a well-regulated militia, as so construed, its prohibition is absolute.

This brings us to the First Amendment. It reads:

Congress shall make no law respecting an establishment of religion,
or prohibiting the free exercise thereof; or abridging the freedom of
speech, or of the press; or the right of the people peaceably to assemble, and to petition the Government for a redress of grievances.

The phrase, "Congress shall make no law" is composed of plain
words, easily understood. The Framers knew this. The language
used by Madison in his proposal was different, but no less emphatic and unequivocal. That proposal is worth reading:

The civil rights of none shall be abridged on account of religious
belief or worship, nor shall any national religion be established,
nor shall the full and equal rights of conscience be in any manner,
or on any pretext, infringed.
"The people shall not be deprived or abridged of their right to
speak, to write, or to publish their sentiments; and the freedom
of the press, as one of the great bulwarks of liberty, shall be in-
violable.
"The people shall not be restrained from peaceably assembling
and consulting for their common good; nor from applying to the
Legislature by petitions, or remonstrances, for redress of their
grievances." [4]

Neither as offered nor as adopted is the language of this Amendment anything less than absolute. Madison was emphatic about
this. He told the Congress that under it "The right of freedom of
speech is secured; the liberty of the press is expressly declared to be
beyond the reach of this Government. . . ." [5] (Emphasis supplied
in all quotations.) Some years later Madison wrote that "it would
seem scarcely possible to doubt that *no power whatever* over the
press was supposed to be delegated by the Constitution, as it originally stood, and that the amendment was intended as a *positive and*

absolute reservation of it." [6] With referenc
ture of the First Amendment's command ag
religious liberty, Madison later said that "the
right in the general government to intermeddl
that "this subject is, for the honor of Americ
unshackled. The *government has no jurisdicti*

To my way of thinking, at least, the history and language of
the Constitution and the Bill of Rights, which I have discussed
with you, make it plain that one of the primary purposes of the
Constitution with its amendments was to withdraw from the
government all power to act in certain areas—whatever the scope
of those areas may be. If I am right in this then there is, at least
in those areas, no justification whatever for "balancing" a particular right against some expressly granted power of Congress.
If the Constitution withdraws from government all power over
subject matter in an area, such as religion, speech, press, assembly,
and petition, there is nothing over which authority may be exerted.

The Framers were well aware that the individual rights they
sought to protect might be easily nullified if subordinated to the
general powers granted to Congress. One of the reasons for adoption of the Bill of Rights was to prevent just that. Specifically the
people feared that the "necessary and proper" clause could be
used to project the generally granted Congressional powers into
the protected areas of individual rights. One need only read the
debates in the various states to find out that this is true. But
if these debates leave any doubt, Mr. Madison's words to Congress
should remove it. In speaking of the necessary and proper clause
and its possible effect on freedom of religion he said, as reported
in the Annals of Congress:

Whether the words are necessary or not, he did not mean to
say, but they had been required by some of the State Conventions,
who seemed to entertain an opinion that under the clause of the
Constitution, which gave power to Congress to make all laws
necessary and proper to carry into execution the Constitution, and
the laws made under it, enabled them to make laws of such a
nature as might infringe the rights of conscience, and establish
a national religion; to prevent these effects he presumed the
amendment was intended, and he thought it as well expressed
as the nature of the language would admit.[8]

...s obvious to me that Congress, in exercising its general
.., is expressly forbidden to use means prohibited by the
of Rights. Whatever else the phrase "necessary and proper"
.ay mean, it must be that Congress may only adopt such means
to carry out its powers as are "proper," that is, not specifically
prohibited.

It has also been argued that since freedom of speech, press,
and religion in England were narrow freedoms at best, and since
there were many English laws infringing those freedoms, our First
Amendment should not be thought to bar similar infringements
by Congress. Again one needs only to look to the debates in
Congress over the First Amendment to find that the First Amendment cannot be treated as a mere codification of English law.
Mr. Madison made a clear explanation to Congress that it was
the purpose of the First Amendment to grant greater protection
than England afforded its citizens. He said:

In the declaration of rights which that country has established,
the truth is, they have gone no farther than to raise a barrier
against the power of the Crown; the power of the Legislature is
left altogether indefinite. Although I know whenever the great
rights, the trial by jury, freedom of the press, or liberty of conscience, came in question in that body, invasion of them is resisted by able advocates, yet their Magna Charta does not contain
any one provision for the security of those rights, respecting which
the people of America are most alarmed. The freedom of the
press and rights of conscience, those choicest privileges of the
people, are unguarded in the British Constitution.
But although the case may be widely different, and it may not
be thought necessary to provide limits for the legislative power in
that country, yet a different opinion prevails in the United States.[9]

It was the desire to give the people of America greater protection against the powerful Federal Government than the English
had had against their government that caused the Framers to put
these freedoms of expression, again in the words of Madison, "beyond the reach of this Government."

When closely analyzed the idea that there can be no "absolute"
constitutional guarantees in the Bill of Rights is frightening to

contemplate even as to individual safeguards in the original Constitution. Take, for instance, the last clause in Article Six that "no religious Test shall ever be required" for a person to hold office in the United States. Suppose Congress should find that some religious sect was dangerous because of its foreign affiliations. Such was the belief on which English test oaths rested for a long time and some of the states had test oaths on that assumption at the time, and after, our Constitution was adopted in 1789. Could Congress, or the Supreme Court, or both, put this precious privilege to be free from test oaths on scales, find it outweighed by some other public interest, and therefore make United States officials and employees swear they did not and never had belonged to or associated with a particular religious group suspected of disloyalty? Can Congress, in the name of over-balancing necessity, suspend habeas corpus in peacetime? Are there circumstances under which Congress could, after nothing more than a legislative bill of attainder, take away a man's life, liberty, or property? Hostility of the Framers toward bills of attainder was so great that they took the unusual step of barring such legislative punishments by the States as well as the Federal Government. They wanted to remove any possibility of such proceedings anywhere in this country. This is not strange in view of the fact that they were much closer than we are to the great Act of Attainder by the Irish Parliament, in 1688, which condemned between two and three thousand men, women, and children to exile or death without anything that even resembled a trial.[10]

Perhaps I can show you the consequences of the balancing approach to the Bill of Rights liberties by a practical demonstration of how it might work. The last clause of the Fifth Amendment is: "nor shall private property be taken for public use, without just compensation." On its face this command looks absolute, but if one believes that it should be weighed against the powers granted to Congress, there might be some circumstances in which this right would have to give way, just as there are some circumstances in which it is said the right of freedom of religion, speech, press, assembly and petition can be balanced away. Let us see how the balancing concept would apply to the just compensation provision of the Bill of Rights in the following wholly imaginary judicial opinion of Judge X:

This case presents an important question of constitutional law. The United States is engaged in a stupendous national defense undertaking which requires the acquisition of much valuable land throughout the country. The plaintiff here owns 500 acres of land. The location of the land gives it a peculiarly strategic value for carrying out the defense program. Due to the great national emergency that exists, Congress concluded that the United States could not afford at this time to pay compensation for the lands which it needed to acquire. For this reason an Act was passed authorizing seizure without compensation of all the lands required for the defense establishment.

In reaching a judgment on this case, I cannot shut my eyes to the fact that the United States is in a desperate condition at this time. Nor can I, under established canons of constitutional construction, invalidate a Congressional enactment if there are any rational grounds upon which Congress could have passed it. I think there are such grounds here. Highly important among the powers granted Congress by the Constitution are the powers to declare war, maintain a navy, and raise and support armies. This, of course, means the power to conduct war successfully. To make sure that Congress is not unduly restricted in the exercise of these constitutional powers, the Constitution also gives Congress power to make all laws 'necessary and proper to carry into execution the foregoing powers. . . .' This necessary and proper clause applies to the powers to make war and support armies as it does to all the other granted powers.

Plaintiff contends, however, that the Fifth Amendment's provision about compensation is so absolute a command that Congress is wholly without authority to violate it, however great this nation's emergency and peril may be. I must reject this contention. We must never forget that it is a constitution we are expounding. And a constitution, unlike ordinary statutes, must endure for ages; it must be adapted to changing conditions and the needs of changing communities. Without such capacity for change, our Constitution would soon be outmoded and become a dead letter. Therefore its words must never be read as rigid absolutes. The Bill of Rights' commands, no more than any others, can stay the hands of Congress from doing that which the general welfare imperatively demands. When two great constitutional provisions like these conflict—as here the power to make war conflicts with the requirements for just compensation—it becomes the duty of courts to weigh the constitutional right of an individual to compensation against the power of Congress to wage a successful war.

While the question is not without doubt, I have no hesitation in finding the challenged Congressional Act valid. Driven by the absolute necessity to protect the nation from foreign aggression, the national debt has risen to billions of dollars. The Government's credit is such that interest rates have soared. Under these circumstances, Congress was rationally entitled to find that if it paid for all the lands it needs it might bankrupt the nation and render it helpless in its hour of greatest need. Weighing as I must the loss the individual will suffer because he has to surrender his land to the nation without compensation against the great public interest in conducting war, I hold the Act valid. A decree will be entered accordingly.

Of course, I would not decide this case this way nor do I think any other judge would so decide it today. My reason for refusing this approach would be that I think the Fifth Amendment's command is absolute and not to be overcome without constitutional amendment even in times of grave emergency. But I think this wholly fictitious opinion fairly illustrates the possibilities of the balancing approach, not only as to the just compensation clause, but as to other provisions of the Bill of Rights as well. The great danger of the judiciary balancing process is that in times of emergency and stress it gives Government the power to do what it thinks necessary to protect itself, regardless of the rights of individuals. If the need is great, the right of Government can always be said to outweigh the rights of the individual. If "balancing" is accepted as the test, it would be hard for any conscientious judge to hold otherwise in times of dire need. And laws adopted in times of dire need are often very hasty and oppressive laws, especially when, as often happens, they are carried over and accepted as normal. Furthermore, the balancing approach to basic individual liberties assumes to legislators and judges more power than either the Framers or I myself believe should be entrusted, without limitation, to any man or any group of men.

It seems to me that the "balancing" approach also disregards all of the unique features of our Constitution which I described earlier. In reality this approach returns us to the state of legislative supremacy which existed in England and which the Framers were so determined to change once and for all. On the one hand, it denies the judiciary its constitutional power to measure acts of Congress by the standards set down in the Bill of Rights. On the other hand, though apparently reducing judicial powers by saying that acts of Congress may be held unconstitutional only when they are found to have no rational legislative basis, this approach really gives the Court, along with Congress, a greater power, that of overriding the plain commands of the Bill of Rights on a find-ing of weighty public interest. In effect, it changes the direction of our form of government from a government of limited powers to a government in which Congress may do anything that Courts believe to be "reasonable."

Of course the decision to provide a constitutional safeguard for a particular right, such as the fair trial requirements of the Fifth and Sixth Amendments and the right of free speech protection of the First, involves a balancing of conflicting interests. Strict procedures may release guilty men; protecting speech and press may involve dangers to a particular government. I believe, however, that the Framers themselves did this balancing when they wrote the Constitution and the Bill of Rights. They appreciated the risks involved and they decided that certain rights should be guaranteed regardless of these risks. Courts have neither the right nor the power to review this original decision of the Framers and to attempt to make a different evaluation of the importance of the rights granted in the Constitution. Where conflicting values exist in the field of individual liberties protected by the Constitution, that document settles the conflict, and its policy should not be changed without constitutional amendments by the people in the manner provided by the people.

Misuse of government power, particularly in times of stress, has brought suffering to humanity in all ages about which we have authentic history. Some of the world's noblest and finest men have suffered ignominy and death for no crime—unless unortho-doxy is a crime. Even enlightened Athens had its victims such as Socrates. Because of the same kind of bigotry, Jesus, the great Dissenter, was put to death on a wooden cross. The flames of inquisitions all over the world have warned that men endowed with unlimited government power, even earnest men, consecrated to a cause, are dangerous.

For my own part, I believe that our Constitution, with its absolute guarantees of individual rights, is the best hope for the aspirations of freedom which men share everywhere. I cannot agree with those who think of the Bill of Rights as an 18th Cen-tury straitjacket, unsuited for this age. It is old but not all old things are bad. The evils it guards against are not only old, they are with us now, they exist today. Almost any morning you open your daily paper you can see where some person somewhere in the world is on trial or has just been convicted of supposed disloyalty to a new group controlling the government which has set out to purge its suspected enemies and all those who had dared to be against its successful march to power. Nearly always you see that these political heretics are being tried by military tribunals or some other summary and sure method for disposition of the accused. Now and then we even see the convicted victims as they march to their execution.

Experience all over the world has demonstrated, I fear, that the distance between stable, orderly government and one that has been taken over by force is not so great as we have assumed. Our own free system to live and progress has to have intelligent citizens, citizens who cannot only think and speak and write to influence people, but citizens who are free to do that without fear of governmental censorship or reprisal.

The provisions of the Bill of Rights that safeguard fair legal procedures came about largely to protect the weak and the oppressed from punishment by the strong and the powerful who wanted to stifle the voices of discontent raised in protest against oppression and injustice in public affairs. Nothing that I have read in the Congressional debates on the Bill of Rights indicates that there was any belief that the First Amendment contained any qualifications. The only arguments that tended to look in this direction at all were those that said "that all paper barriers against the power of the Community are too weak to be worthy of attention." Suggestions were also made in and out of Congress that a Bill of Rights would be a futile gesture since there would be no way to enforce the safeguards for freedom it provided. Mr. Madison answered this argument in these words:

If they [the Bill of Rights amendments] are incorporated into the Constitution, independent tribunals of justice will consider themselves in a peculiar manner the guardians of those rights; they will be an impenetrable bulwark against any assumption of power in the Legislative or Executive; they will be naturally led to resist every encroachment upon rights expressly stipulated for in the Constitution by the declaration of rights.[11]

I fail to see how courts can escape this sacred trust.

Since the earliest days philosophers have dreamed of a country where the mind and spirit of man would be free; where there would be no limits to inquiry; where men would be free to explore the unknown and to challenge the most deeply rooted beliefs and principles. Our First Amendment was a bold effort to adopt this principle—to establish a country with no legal restrictions of any kind upon the subjects people could investigate, discuss and deny. The Framers knew, better perhaps than we do today, the risks they were taking. They knew that free speech might be the friend of change and revolution. But they also knew that it is always the deadliest enemy of tyranny. With this knowledge they still believed that the ultimate happiness and security of a nation lies in its ability to explore, to change, to grow and ceaselessly to adapt itself to new knowledge born of inquiry free from any kind of governmental control over the mind and spirit of man. Loyalty comes from love of good government, not fear of a bad one.

The First Amendment is truly the heart of the Bill of Rights. The Framers balanced its freedoms of religion, speech, press, assembly and petition against the needs of a powerful central government, and decided that in those freedoms lies this nation's only true security. They were not afraid for men to be free. We should not be. . . .

REFERENCES

[1] 1 Rives, Madison 44 (1859).
[2] 4 Jefferson, Writings 505, 506 (Washington ed. 1861).
[3] 1 Annals of Cong. 437.
[4] 1 Annals 434.
[5] 1 Annals of Cong. 738.
[6] 6 Madison, Writings, 341, 391 (Hunt ed. 1906).
[7] See Everson v. Board of Education, 330 U. S. 1, 38.
[8] 1 Annals of Cong. 730.
[9] 1 Annals of Cong. 436.
[10] See Joint Anti-Fascist Refugee Committee v. McGrath, 341 U. S. 123, 146.
[11] 1 Annals of Cong. 439.

Selected Bibliography

Burton, Harold H., Associate Justice, 1945-1958
"The Keystone of our Freedom—an Independent Judiciary," 39 *American Bar Association Journal* 1067 (1953)

Clark, Tom C., Associate Justice, 1949—
"The Supreme Court as a Protector of Liberty Under the Rule of Law," 43 *Marquette Law Review* 11 (1959)
"Constitutional Adjudication and the Supreme Court," 9 *Drake Law Review* 59 (1960)

Douglas, William O., Associate Justice, 1939—
"Procedural Safeguards in the Bill of Rights," 31 *Journal of the American Judicature Society* 166 (1948)
We the Judges, Garden City, N. Y., Doubleday, 1954
"The Supreme Court and its Case Load," 45 *Cornell Law Quarterly* 401 (1960)

Frankfurter, Felix, Associate Justice, 1939—
"The Job of a Supreme Court Justice," *New York Times Magazine*, Nov. 28, 1954
Of Law and Men: Papers and Addresses, 1939-1956, N. Y., Harcourt, Brace, 1956
"The Supreme Court in the Mirror of the Justices," 105 *U. of Pa. Law Review* 781 (1957)

Harlan, John M., Associate Justice, 1955—
"Manning the Dikes," 13 *The Record of the Association of the Bar of the City of New York* 541 (1958)
"Some Aspects of the Judicial Process in the Supreme Court of the United States," 33 *Australian Law Journal* 108 (1959)

Hughes, Charles Evans, Associate Justice, 1910-1916; Chief Justice, 1930-1941
The Supreme Court of the United States, N. Y., Columbia Univ., 1928

Jackson, Robert H., Associate Justice, 1941-1954
"The Meaning of Statutes: What Congress Says or What the Court Says," 34 *American Bar Association Journal* 535 (1948)

"The Role of the Judiciary in Maintaining Our Liberties," 39 *American Bar Association Journal* 961 (1953)
The Supreme Court in the American System of Government, Cambridge, Mass., Harvard Univ., 1955

Reed, Stanley, Associate Justice, 1938-1957
"Law and Society: Fixed Principles and Changing Applications," State Bar of California, Monterey, Oct. 3, 1957.

Roberts, Owen D., Associate Justice, 1930-1945
"American Constitutional Government," in *The Court and the Constitution*, Boston, Boston Univ., 1953

Rutledge, Wiley B., Associate Justice, 1943-1949
A Declaration of Legal Faith, Lawrence, Kans., Univ. of Kansas, 1947

Stone, Harlan F., Associate Justice, 1925-1941; Chief Justice, 1941-1946
"Fifty Years' Work of the United States Supreme Court," 14 *American Bar Association Journal* 428 (1929)
"Dissenting Opinions Are Not Without Value," 26 *Journal of the American Judicature Society* 63 (1942)

Vinson, Fred M., Chief Justice, 1946-1953
"Our Enduring Constitution," 6 *Washington and Lee Law Review* 1 (1949)

Warren, Earl, Chief Justice, 1953—
"The Law and the Future," *Fortune* Magazine, November 1955
"The Blessings of Liberty," 1955 Washington Univ. Law Quarterly 105 (1955)
The Public Papers of Chief Justice Earl Warren, N. Y., Simon and Schuster, 1959